TABLE OF CONTENTS

TABLE OF CONTENTS v

TABLE OF FIGURES vii

INTRODUCTION 1

   The Counterinsurgency Environment 2

      Describing The Current Environment 3

      The Evolving Nature Of Insurgency 7

   Definitions 9

THEORETICAL AND DOCTRINAL FOUNDATIONS 11

   Operational Art 11

      The Roots of Operational Art 11

      The Levels of War 12

      Integration in US Doctrine 13

   The Campaign and Operational Design 14

      The Joint Campaign Planning Model 17

   Counterinsurgency 18

      Counterinsurgency Theory and Literature 19

      US Counterinsurgency Doctrine 24

   Conclusion 26

THE HUKBALAHAP IN THE PHILIPPINES 27

   Background 27

      Demographic and Geographic Overview of the Philippines 27

      Historic Perspective 28

      The Philippines Communist Party and the Huks 29

      Ramon Magsaysay 32

   The Conduct of Insurgency and Counterinsurgency in the Phillipines 33

      First Phase: Imminent Collapse 33

      Second Phase: Seizing the Initiative and Defeating the Huks 35

   The United States' Strategic Objectives for the Philippines 39

   The Campaign Plan in the Philippines 39

   Conclusion 42

EL SALVADOR, 1981-1992 42

   Background 43

      Demographic and Geographic Overview of El Salvador 43

      Historical Perspective 43

      The Road to Insurgency 44

   The Conduct of Insurgency and Counterinsurgency in El Salvador 46

   Analysis of Campaign Planning in El Salvador 50

      The Woerner Report (1981) 51

      The National Campaign Plan (1983) 54

      Unidos Para Reconstruir (1986) 57

   Conclusions 58

COMPARATIVE ANALYSIS OF THE COUNTERINSURGENCY CAMPAIGNS 60

   Similarities 60

      Criticality of US Advisory Assistance and Aid 60

      Use of Aid as Leverage to Promote US Strategic Goals 61

      The Effect of Honest, Free Elections 62

      Protracted Nature of the Conflicts 63

Dissimilarities..63
    Emergence of a Leader...63
    Reintegration of Insurgents into Society and the Respect of Human Rights.........................64
    Political Power of the Armed Forces..65
    External Support of the Insurgency..66
    Immediate Strategic Guidance..67
  Conclusion...67
CONCLUSIONS AND RECOMMENDATIONS...68
  General Conclusions 68
  Specific Conclusions 68
    Integrated Campaign Plan at the Operational Level..68
    Operational Art for Counterinsurgency 69
    Long Term Commitment...70
    Aid for Access and Leverage..70
  Recommendations 71
    Further Study of Counterinsurgency in Terms of Operational Art...71
    Situational Understanding of the Operational Environment..71
    Defining Progress in Counterinsurgency 72
    Victory in Counterinsurgency 72
    Effects-Based Operations for Counterinsurgency..73
  The Future of Counterinsurgency Campaign Planning..74
Appendix A: The Facets of Operational Art..75
Appendix B: Internal Defense and Development Strategy Model..76
BIBLIOGRAPHY..77

TABLE OF FIGURES

Figure 1: The Facets of Operational Art 75
Figure 2: Internal Defense and Development Strategy Model 76

INTRODUCTION

> Here, on 26 July 1972 the Royal Thai Army burned all its American textbooks. From this dates our victory over the communists. [Inscription over the incinerator in the Royal Thai Army Headquarters][1]

The United States (US) has conducted or supported more than a dozen counterinsurgencies in the 20th century. The current global war on terrorism might also be viewed as a counterinsurgency (COIN) since it involves the military, paramilitary, political, economic, psychological, informational and civic actions of the US employed to protect the legitimacy of its political community, political system, authorities and policies from an overt threat applying political resources and violence.[2] The emerging strategic environment indicates that the US will be involved with counterinsurgencies in the future and there appear to exist operational shortfalls in the knowledge, planning, and execution of COIN.

The nature of COIN is complex. Politics and policy generally play a primary role. Counterinsurgencies involving the United States inherently include multinational and interagency players, and the military typically plays a supporting role.[3] The nature of insurgency continues to evolve and adapt as well. To manage the increasing complexity of the COIN environment, a coherent planning model is needed in order to achieve ultimate success. This model must link strategic aims with tactical actions. The joint campaign planning model may provide an appropriate means to bridge these shortfalls.

Do sound frameworks exist in current joint or service doctrine (and subsequently in practice) for COIN and campaign planning, or is it necessary to "burn the books" like the Thais in order to find success? Perhaps operational COIN planning previously existed, but is a skill that needs to be relearned. As aptly stated in an early issue of *Combat Information*, a training bulletin

---

[1] Stuart Slade, "Successful Counter-insurgency: How Thais Burnt the Books and Beat the Guerillas," *Internal Security & CO-IN,* an editorial supplement to *International Defense Review 22,* (October 1989): 21.

[2] Joint Publication 1-02. *Department of Defense Dictionary of Military and Associated Terms.* (23 March 1994 as amended through 1 September 2000), 112; Bard E. O'Neill, *Insurgency & Terrorism: Inside Modern Revolutionary Warfare* (Dulles: Brassey's (US), Inc., 1990), 13.

1

used to pass US Army lessons learned during the Korean War,[4] American doctrine was generally sound but, "The one great lesson that can be learned...is that these [US doctrine, tactics, techniques, organization and equipment] must be applied with vigor, imagination and intelligence."[5] This monograph examines whether the current joint campaign planning model adequately addresses existing operational shortfalls in COIN planning.

To answer this question, the COIN environment is defined through an examination of the current operating environment and the nature of insurgency. COIN theory and current US doctrine are evaluated in order to demonstrate that operational shortfalls exist. Operational art and campaign planning are examined and discussed to provide a basis of evaluation of planning shortfalls. Two historical case studies (The Philippines, 1948-1954, and El Salvador, 1980-1992) are presented in order to illustrate and analyze COIN doctrine and campaign planning methodologies and their relative success or failure in the overall conduct of the counterinsurgencies. The final result of this research is general and specific conclusions on the adequacy of the current campaign planning model for COIN and recommendations for improvement or modification of the process.

The Counterinsurgency Environment

> There has been a quiet revolution in strategy over the last half-century, moving with the same speed but much less visibility than the breakthroughs in military technology. This revolution is in the theory and practice of low-intensity warfare, as the rise and perfection of revolutionary war demonstrate. If there is anything distinctively new about the post-World War II environment, it can be found at the extreme ends of the conflict spectrum, in nuclear strategy as well as LIC [Low Intensity Conflict].
>
> -Thomas A. Grant[6]

---

[3] Joint Publication 3-07. *Joint Doctrine for Military Operations Other than War.* (16 June 1995), I-2, I-6.
[4] Jay Luvaas, "Lessons and Lessons Learned: A Historical Perspective," in *The Lessons of Recent Wars in the Third World, Volume I,* ed. Robert E. Harkavy and Stephanie G. Neuman (Lexington: Lexington Books, 1985), 66.
[5] Office of the Chief of Army Field Forces, Fort Monroe, Virginia. *Combat Information,* Training Bulletin No.5, 27 September 1951, 1; quoted in Jay Luvaas, "Lessons and Lessons Learned: A Historical Perspective," in *The Lessons of Recent Wars in the Third World, Volume I,* ed. Robert E. Harkavy and Stephanie G. Neuman (Lexington: Lexington Books, 1985), 51-72, 66.
[6] Thomas A. Grant, "Government, Politics, and Low-Intensity Conflict," in *Low-Intensity Conflict: Old Threats in a New World,* ed. Edwin G. Corr and Stephan Sloan, Westview Studies in Regional Security, ed. Wm. J. Olson (Boulder: Westview Press, 1992), 258.

This section provides a brief overview of the current and emerging security environment and significant factors that create and sustain opportunity for insurgency. The evolving and adaptive nature of insurgency is also examined with particular emphasis on the modern era and evolutionary changes since the end of the Cold War.

Describing The Current Environment

Flux in the strategic environment caused by the end of the Cold War, combined with other accelerators, like population growth and urbanization, globalization and the information revolution to mention but a few, has created a world that has seen an increase of massive proportions and numbers in US military deployments and interventions in military operations other than war (MOOTW) (or in its current and reemergent US Army incantation, stability operations[7] and support operations). In fact, US policy makers appear to be taking a new and significantly Clausewitzian view of the threat and use of force "as an integral part of political strategy" versus the more traditional use of force only as last resort.[8] Many of these deployments were in support of COIN (if not necessarily in name, at least in definition). With ongoing foreign internal defense (FID) operations worldwide, there are significant indications that the pace of these deployments will not decrease, but in fact, increase.

Some of the effects of the fall of the Soviet Union were a loosening of internal and external political and social controls in formerly Soviet aligned countries, and an increase in the availability of modern weaponry, mainly from former Eastern Bloc nations, in return for needed hard currency. There is also a growing trend to recognize national/ethnic determinism over state sovereignty. Thus, the international community generally favors interventions supporting ethnic

---

[7] The term stability operations was used by the US Army to cover the same general range of operations in the late 1960's, appearing in the 1968 edition of FM 100-5 *Operations* as well as having its own manual, FM 31-23 *Stability Operations*, which was issued in 1967.

[8] James A. Winnefeld and others, *Intervention in Intrastate Conflict: Implications for the Army in the Post-Cold War Era* (Santa Monica: RAND, 1995, MR-554/1-A), 40.

self determination, even at the expense of the sovereignty of an existing nation state.[9] The creation of an "ideological vacuum" following the discreditment of the Soviet system of government has also occurred. The vacuum encouraged less developed societies to embrace religious fundamentalism or ethnic self awareness as a means to obtain a sovereign identity due to their inability to adjust to the dominant world paradigm of western democracy and free market capitalism.[10] Additional strain was added to the "new world order" in the social, economic and political arena through rapid growth in population and urbanization in the underdeveloped world, globalization and the information revolution. How these factors facilitate social unrest is addressed in the following paragraphs.

Population growth continues to be a factor of instability and discontent in the less developed world. By 2050, the US Census Bureau estimates the world population will exceed nine billion, or a nearly fifty percent increase over the current global population. Today, 99 percent of all net annual gain of world population occurs in the developing world (96 percent in the developing regions of Africa, Asia and Latin America), and by 2020, all net gain will be recorded from developing countries.[11] In these developing countries, the majority of this population gain will be in urban areas, exacerbating the problem of urbanization.

Urbanization refers to the increasing migration of people from rural to urban areas, both in total amount as well as in rate. In 1950, the first year statistics were kept, approximately thirty percent of the world's population lived in urban areas. By 2025, that will increase to fifty eight percent. In less developed countries, the urban population is expected to double between 2000 and 2025, creating an urban population in excess of 3.5 billion, and surpass the rural population

---

[9] Ibid., 23.
[10] Ibid., 14-15.
[11] U.S. Census Bureau, "World Population Profile: 1998 – Highlights" site at http://www.census.gov/ipc/www/wp98001.html, accessed on 12 December 2002.

4

by 2020.[12] Rate and scale also play a factor in the developing world, such that not only is urbanization more rapid, there is also expected phenomenal growth of cities of a million people or more (in excess of 100 percent by 2015).[13] Several factors, addressed below, are linked to urbanization and create exploitable situations of societal discontent, often leading to civil violence to a scale creating state and societal instability. Urban poverty, unemployment or underemployment, and decaying or overtaxed infrastructure lead to failures in meeting basic needs of the urban population, particularly in terms of housing, electricity or water. The transition from rural to urban areas may promote the breakdown of extended family systems, and create greater community isolation and social dislocation. Cities in less developed countries are also hotbeds of infectious disease, most notably HIV/AIDS, and are generally hazardous to their inhabitants in terms of both natural disasters and environmental hazards.

Globalization refers to the integration of the world's economies. While considered an overall historical process, modern globalization is strongly driven by the information revolution, which has allowed integration of world financial markets. In strictly economic terms, there are four major factors of globalization: trade, movement of capital, movement of people, and movement of information. Also significant in globalization are a broader spectrum of environmental, social, cultural and political effects due to economic integration.[14]

In theory, globalization creates economic efficiency through open global markets, which enhance competition and a devise a coherent division of labor. However, the global market does not ensure that all participants share the benefits of this efficiency equitably. While there was enormous growth in overall global income and gross domestic product during the later half of the 20th century, the gap in the distribution of income among countries, as well as among individuals,

---

[12] Martin P.Brockerhoff, "An Urbanizing World," *Population Bulletin* 55, No. 3, (September 2000), 48 pages, site at http://www.prb.org/Template.cfm?Section=RB&template=/ContentManagement/Content Display.cfm&ContentID=5886, accessed on 12 December 2002, 3-4.
[13] Ibid., 7.

has increased dramatically.[15] While globalization may not be the sole cause of this income gap, it provides a ready and continuing source of social discontent.

The information revolution is a driving force in globalization, not just in the economic arena, but in the social, cultural and political arenas as well. The information revolution has been created by modern information and communication technologies, as well as cultural changes, giving rise to phenomena like the Internet and global 24-hour news networks. The information revolution has greatly enhanced the informational element of national power, especially in the United States. It also creates a number of vulnerabilities and drawbacks, not least among them, the seeming requirement of instantaneous response by policy makers in answer to public opinion molded through the massive and immediate transmission of media content without analysis.

The information revolution acts as an accelerator to social discontent in terms of Ted Robert Gurr's concept of "perceived relative deprivation."[16] Gurr's concept describes a gap between a society's expectations and its capability to meet them. Significant to this concept is not merely the gap itself, but the rate at which it changes. The information revolution has led to a massive export of Western culture, which can give rise to a growing and serious unbalance in expectations and capabilities in lesser developed countries. In fact, it can create social discontent among reformers as well as traditionalists.

The majority of modern conflict is occurring intrastate versus interstate, that is to say, internal war or insurgency. The linkages between nation states caused by globalization and the information revolution makes interstate warfare less likely and less sustainable. Combatants in intrastate warfare are taking on different strategies, as well as different organizational structures. Warlordism, constant low level violence, lawlessness, religious extremism, state failure, and ethnic and tribal conflict abound, causing further problems in human migration.

---

[14] International Monetary Fund Staff, "Globalization: Threat or Opportunity?" April 12, 2000 (Corrected January 2002), Site at http://www.imf.org/external/np/exr/ ib/2000/ 041200.htm, accessed on 30 December 2002.
[15] Ibid.

To briefly illustrate the scope of intrastate conflict, as well as an increasing trend of interventions, ongoing conflicts, and peacekeeping missions will be examined. The Institute for International Mediation and Conflict Resolution (IIMCR) counts 26 ongoing "high intensity" conflicts (greater than 1000 deaths per year) with only 4 of these being interstate. Additionally, there are 78 "low intensity" conflicts (between 100 and 1,000 deaths per year) and over 170 "political violence" conflicts (less than 100 deaths per year). There are currently 58 ongoing peace missions.

The Evolving Nature Of Insurgency

Throughout history, insurgency has been one of the most prevalent forms of warfare and has shown considerable evolution and adaptation both in tactics, techniques and procedures, but also in terms of motivations. This was expressed by Shy and Collier who stated, "revolutions, by definition, are not made by states and their bureaucracies, but by raw social energies, directed by leaders who must improvise, adapt quickly, and often act before they have time to think, if they are to win or even survive."[17] Insurgency has been the traditional way a weaker group has attempted to redress actual or perceived wrongs against a ruling faction or an occupying power.

The post World War II era saw the emergence of politically-inspired insurgency, generally referred to as "revolutionary war," in response to the death of colonialism and the bipolar nature of the global security environment. Revolutionary war, using force to seize power in order to forge radical political and social change, was generally inspired by Mao Zedong's theory of protracted people's war. Others, like Che Guevara, and Guillén and Marighella, added to the body of politically inspired insurgency strategies.

However, the end of the Cold War has marked a new chapter in insurgency. Steven Metz states, "To transcend the conceptual limits of the Cold War, insurgency should be considered as simply protracted, organized violence - whether revolutionary or nonrevolutionary, political or

---

[16] Ted Robert Gurr, *Why Men Rebel*, (Princeton: Princeton University Press, 1970).

nonpolitical, and open or clandestine - which threatens security and requires a government response."[18] Revolutionary war still exists, but not in the predominance found during the bipolar struggle between the West and the Soviets. New forms of insurgency have emerged as well as more traditional forms adapted to present conditions. Ian Beckett refers to these adapted forms as "forward to the past" and elegantly states "the past of guerilla warfare and insurgency represents both the shadow of things that have been and those that will be."[19] In large part, Beckett refers to the reemergence of warlordism, ethnic and tribal warfare, and religious fundamentalism and fanaticism as sources of internal conflict. Goals of these insurgencies may differ significantly from "revolutionary war," since neither protraction nor legitimacy may be a goal, but the seizure of territory and the physical elimination of those dissimilar to the insurgent might be.

Nearly eight years ago, Dr Steven Metz described two emerging forms of insurgency. The first was commercial insurgency, which poses threats to security and stability without necessarily attempting to seize the power of the state. Commercial insurgency is essentially "powerful criminal organizations with a political veneer and the ability to threaten national security instead of just law and order."[20] The obvious manifestation is narcoinsurgency, primarily in Latin America and Asia, but commercial insurgency has also appeared in Africa, primarily regarding gems and precious metals. Commercial insurgencies can often be transnational and are differentiated from traditional organized crime by their political aspects. In some cases, these insurgencies are marriages of necessity due to the loss of funding and external support caused by the end of the Cold War. The other form of particular impact, based on the current number of UN and multilateral peace missions, was "aimed at multinational political organizations and military

---

[17] John Shy and Thomas W. Collier, "Revolutionary Warfare," in *Makers of Modern Strategy: From Machiavelli to the Nuclear Age*, ed. Peter Paret, (Princeton: Princeton University Press, 1986), 819.
[18] Steven Metz, "A Flame Kept Burning: Counterinsurgency Support After the Cold War," *Parameters* 25, no. 3, (Autumn 1995): 36.
[19] Ian Beckett, "Forward to the Past: Insurgency in Our Midst," *Harvard International Review* 23, no. 2 (Summer 2001): 63.
[20] Steven Metz, "A Flame Kept Burning: Counterinsurgency Support After the Cold War," 33. See also Steven Metz, *The Future of Insurgency* and *Counterinsurgency: Strategy and the Phoenix of American Capability,* (Carlisle Barracks: Strategic Studies Institute, U.S. Army War College, 28 February 1995)

forces attempting to stabilize failed states."[21] The primary example of this type of insurgency is Somalia, but has certainly also manifested in the Balkans, as well as in Afghanistan after the fall of the Taliban.

Definitions

The following definitions will apply throughout this research project

Campaign: "A series of related joint major operations that arrange tactical, operational, and strategic actions to accomplish strategic and operational objectives within a given time and space."[22]

Counterinsurgency (COIN): Joint Publication 1-02 defines COIN as "those military, paramilitary, political, economic, psychological and civic actions taken by a government to defeat an insurgency."[23] There are two significant problems with this definition: the requirement of a nation state to conduct COIN ignores the increasingly transnational nature of modern insurgency and it fails to explicitly include informational aspects of national power. The definition to be used in this study will be based on the joint definition with the two aspects above addressed and combined, in part, with the definition of insurgency provided by O'Neill (see below). Therefore, COIN in the context of this paper is defined as those military, paramilitary, political, economic, informational actions taken by the ruling authorities to defeat an insurgency and sustain political legitimacy.

Foreign Internal Defense (FID): "Participation by civilian and military agencies of a government in any of the action programs taken by another government to free and protect its society from subversion, lawlessness, and insurgency. Also called FID."[24]

Insurgency: Joint Publication 1-02, provides the official Department of Defense definition of insurgency which is "an organized movement aimed at the overthrow of a

---

[21] Steven Metz, *Counterinsurgency: Strategy and the Phoenix of American Capability,"* 23.

[22] Joint Publication 5-0, *Doctrine for Planning Joint Operations,* (13 April 1995), II-18.

[23] Joint Publication 1-02, 112.

[24] Ibid., 208.

9

constituted government through the use of subversion and armed conflict."[25] This traditional

definition of insurgency is too restricted and does not address the nature of modern insurgency.

On the opposite end of the scale, Steven Metz suggests insurgency is "simply protracted,

organized violence…which threatens security and requires a government response."[26] This

provides greater latitude in recognizing emerging forms and evolution in insurgency, but is too

broad in scope. The definition to be used in this monograph is from Bard O'Neill's *Insurgency*

and Terrorism. He defines insurgency as "a struggle between a nonruling group and the ruling

authorities in which the nonruling group consciously uses *political resources* (e.g., organizational

expertise, propaganda and demonstrations) and violence to destroy, reformulate, or sustain the

basis of legitimacy of one or more aspects of politics."[27]

Internal Defense and Development (IDAD): "The full range of measures taken by a

nation to promote its growth and to protect itself from subversion, lawlessness, and insurgency. It

focuses on building viable institutions (political, economic, social, and military) that respond to

the needs of society. Also called IDAD."[28]

Operational Art: "The employment of military forces to attain strategic and/or

operational objectives through the design, organization, integration, and conduct of strategies,

campaigns, major operations, and battles. Operational art translates the joint force commander's

strategy into operational design and, ultimately, tactical action, by integrating the key activities at

all levels of war."[29]

Operational Design: "The key considerations used as a framework in the course of

planning for a campaign or major operation."[30]

Politics: Using O'Neill's definition of insurgency requires the definition of the aspects of

politics referred to therein. Politics itself is "the process of making and executing binding

---

[25] Ibid., 228.
[26] . Steven Metz, "A Flame Kept Burning: Counterinsurgency Support After the Cold War," 36.
[27] O'Neill, 13.
[28] Joint Publication 1-02, 265.
[29] Ibid., 383.

decisions for society" and the four aspects of politics are, "the political community, the political system, the authorities, and policies."[31]

THEORETICAL AND DOCTRINAL FOUNDATIONS

Operational Art

The language of operational art and the operational level of command is that of high intensity conflict.

-M.I. Laurie[32]

This section briefly addresses the historical roots of operational art, the levels of war and the recognition of operational art by the US armed forces. A basic knowledge of operational art is critical to understanding the design of campaigns and major operations.

The Roots of Operational Art

The term and concept of operational art was introduced by the Russian military theorist Aleksandr A. Svechin in a series of lectures at the Military Academy of the Workers' and Peasants' Red Army during 1923 and 1924.[33] Svechin further elaborated his concept in his book *Strategy*, originally published in 1926. He felt the requirements of modern warfare forced the recognition of three stages to classify military practice. These were tactics, operations and strategy, or what we recognize today as the levels of war. Operational art provides the linkage between combat operations at the tactical level and the overarching war aims of the strategic level. For Svechin, the necessity for operational art was created by the inability to reach a decisive Napoleonic-like victory in modern times where the result of a battle determined the outcome of a war. In large part, this was due to technological innovation, increased battlefield

---

[30] Ibid., 384.

[31] O'Neill, 13.

[32] M.I. Laurie, "The Operational Level in Low Intensity Conflict," *Low Intensity Conflict and Law Enforcement* 1, no. 3 (Winter 1992): 312.

[33] Jacob W. Kipp, "General-Major A. A. Svechin and Modern Warfare: Military History and Military Theory," in *Strategy*, Aleksandr A.Svechin, ed. Kent D. Lee, 23-56 (Minneapolis: East View Publications, 1992), 37-38.

lethality, the drastic increase in the size of armies and the expanded geographic scale in which warfare was conducted in the early twentieth century. Achieving the strategic goal required the logical linkage of a number operations, that is to say a campaign, or as Svechin stated, "this path to the ultimate goal is broken down into a series of operations separated by more or less lengthy pauses, which take place in different areas in a theater and differ significantly from one another due to the differences between the immediate goals one's forces temporarily strive for."[34] Operational art, as distinct from tactics, requires planning, tactics and logistics, with logistics playing an equal or dominant role.

The Levels of War

Current joint doctrine provides a perspective, the three levels of war, in order to illustrate the connectivity between strategic aims and tactical action. The levels of war, like Svechin's, are the strategic, operational and tactical, and apply across the full spectrum of conflict. The strategic level of war is where a nation state articulates national or multilateral security objectives and then dedicates and applies national level resources to accomplish the objectives. The operational level of war links a nation's strategic objectives to the tactical employment of its forces. Operational art is this level's focus. It is also where commanders plan and allocate resources through the operational design of campaigns and major operations. These campaigns or major operations shape the conditions for tactical victory, in order to achieve strategic and operational objectives. The importance of operational art is such that without it, "war would be a set of disconnected engagements, with relative attrition the only measure of success or failure."[35] The tactical level of war is the most familiar to both military and nonmilitary audiences. It involves the employment of units through ordered arrangement and maneuver in relation to friendly, enemy, and civilian elements, and is generally visualized as combat.

---

[34] Aleksandr A. Svechin, *Strategy*, ed. Kent D. Lee. (Minneapolis: East View Publications, 1992), 68-69.
[35] Joint Publication 3-0, *Doctrine for Joint Operations*, (10 September 2001), II-3.

Integration in US Doctrine

The appreciation of operational art, though manifested at times by American military commanders, was not formally recognized and codified until the 1980s. The 1982 edition of US Army's Field Manual (FM) 100-5, *Operations*, identified the operational level of war for the first time. The 1986 edition of FM 100-5 defined and used the term operational art. Shimon Naveh, in his *In Pursuit of Military Excellence: The Evolution of Operational Theory*, states the 1986 edition of FM 100-5 was the "perceptional breakthrough" in American recognition and acceptance of operational art since it "marked the definite recognition of *creativity*, as the basic quality required from operational commanders."[36] The other aspect allowing appreciation of operational art by the US military, according to Naveh, was the recognition of the existence of a "cognitive tension" created by the intangibly defined objectives of the strategic level and the required mechanical execution of the tactical level, which required operational art to fuse them into a "functional formula."[37] Operational art thus provides the basis of planning and executing operations and campaign plans through creatively fusing strategic aims and tactical actions into a "functional formula."

The US joint community also accepted the concept of operational art and promulgated it through joint doctrine. As Colonel (US Army) James Greer, current director of the School for Advanced Military Studies (SAMS) states, "The logic and necessity of the argument for operational art was so compelling that the joint community incorporated virtually intact the Army's doctrine into Joint Publication (JP) 3-0, *Doctrine for Joint Operations*."[38] The appreciation of operational art lead to significant thought and action in the US military, to include the creation of SAMS in 1984, and publications like the Air University Press' *The Air Campaign*

---

[36] Shimon Naveh, *In Pursuit of Military Excellence: The Evolution of Operational Theory,* (London: Frank Cass, 1997), 12.
[37] Ibid., 7.
[38] James K. Greer, "Operational Art for the Objective Force," *Military Review* 82, no. 5 (October 2002): 22.

and the Army War College's study *Campaign Planning*.[39] However, even with the acceptance of

the concept of operational art and considerable intellectual ferment within the services, for over a

decade the joint community was unable to establish, agree upon, articulate, and publish a joint

campaign planning model. A joint doctrine manual and subsequently a joint tactics, techniques

and procedures (JTTP) manual for campaign planning were drafted in 1992 and 1993,

respectively, but never approved.[40] Finally, JP 5-00.1, *Joint Doctrine for Campaign Planning*,

was published in January 2002, and a process of operational design was articulated in a joint

campaign planning model. However, JP 5-00.1 is viewed as interim doctrine to be superceded by

the publication of a new edition of JP 5-0, *Doctrine for Joint Planning Operations*, with the

second draft released 10 December 2002.

The Campaign and Operational Design

In broad terms, operational planners and commanders begin with a clean sheet of paper.
They often define an area of operations (AO), estimate forces required, and evaluate the
requirements for the operation. In contrast, tactical planning proceeds from an existing
operational design.
-FM 5-0 (Final Draft), *Army Planning and Orders Production*[41]

One of his problems is to keep his mind open, to avoid confusing necessary firmness
with stubborn preconception or unreasoning prejudice…. A sound battle plan provides
flexibility in both space and time to meet the constantly changing factors of the battle
problem in such a way as to achieve the final goal of the commander. Rigidity
inevitably invites defeat…
-Dwight D. Eisenhower, *Crusade in Europe*[42]

"A campaign is a series of related major operations that arrange tactical, operational, and

strategic actions to accomplish strategic and operational objectives within a given time and

space."[43] A campaign plan articulates how these major operations are related, resourced and

sequenced in order to achieve the strategic or operational objectives at an acceptable level of risk.

---

[39] Both mentioned items were originally published in 1988.

[40] The semantic change is significant since joint doctrine provides fundamental principles to guide force employment while a JTTP only provides actions and methods that implement joint doctrine.

[41] Field Manual 5-0 (Final Draft), *Army Planning and Orders Production*, (15 July 2002), 1-11.

[42] Dwight D. Eisenhower, *Crusade in Europe*, (Garden City: Doubleday and Company, Inc., 1948; reprint, Pennington: Collectors Reprints, Inc., 1996), 256 (page citations are to the reprint edition).

Campaign planning, or operational design, is the art and science of creatively visualizing operational concepts, which translate strategic aims through the development of a campaign plan. "While facilitated by such procedures as the Joint Operations Planning and Execution System (JOPES) and commonly accepted military decision making models, the operational design process is primarily an intellectual exercise based on experience and judgment."[44]

The considerations for developing a campaign plan are: determining objectives/end states (military, political, social, economic conditions) to achieve the strategic goals (ends); determining a logical action sequence to reach the objectives (ways); determining resource allocation to support the action sequence (means); and finally, determining an acceptable level of cost or risk which allows the achievement of the ends.[45] The result of the operational design process is the conceptual linkage of all the above.

The elements of operational design provide the operational planner a tool set with which to visualize the campaign and articulate the commander's intent.[46] These elements generally include the facets of operational art listed in Joint Publication 3-0, *Doctrine for Joint Operations* (See Appendix A for the complete list). The most commonly recognized and important elements in the current operational design process are end state and center of gravity (COG).

The end state defines the required conditions which achieve the overarching strategic or operational goal. The determination of objectives/end states to reach a strategic or operational goal is critical since this forms the basis of all further planning and presumes adequate guidance from military and civilian policymakers has been provided to define the strategic goals. The understanding of the strategic goal is also essential in ensuring the linkage of the military campaign with efforts to exercise other instruments of national power.

---

[43] Joint Publication 5-0, II-18.
[44] Joint Publication 5-00.1, *Joint Doctrine for Campaign Planning,* (25 January 2002), II-1.
[45] Ibid., I-3-I-4.
[46] Ibid., II-1.

A COG is "those characteristics, capabilities, or sources of power from which a military force derives its freedom of action, physical strength or will to fight."[47] The correct determination of the enemy and friendly COGs significantly drive the direction of a campaign. Both friendly and enemy COGs need to be tested for validity to ensure that an adverse effect on the COG will result in significant changes to a course of action or in the denial of strategic goals.[48] Accurate analysis of the enemy's COGs should identify a mechanism with which to defeat the enemy, as well as suggest lines of operation with which to achieve this defeat. Accurate analysis of friendly COGs, in conjunction with enemy COG analysis, provides guidance on the level of operational protection required by the friendly elements.

There are alternative and emerging operational design concepts currently being explored in their base forms or in combination with each other. These include: the current Army design concept reviewed with enough mental flexibility to encompass full spectrum operations; a systems theory, or gestalt approach, viewing organizations and conflicts as complex adaptive systems and focusing on creating a relative system efficiency advantage between opponents; the effects based operations (EBO) concept where specified actions create outcomes, events or consequences within a system that impact directly on the achievement of an end state; the United States Marine Corps (USMC) complementary design concept of centers of gravity (COG) and critical vulnerabilities (CV) where the means to attack an enemy are viewed from a perspective seeking sources of strength and weakness, respectively; and, an interagency operational design concept which fully integrates the elements of national power at the operational level of war.[49] These concepts will be examined throughout this monograph as they apply to COIN.

---

[47] Ibid., GL-5.

[48] Ibid., II-10.

[49] Greer, 26. For more information on the above concepts see: FM 3-0, *Operations* (14 JUNE 2001) for the Army; John Holland, *Hidden Order: How Adaptation Builds Complexity,* (Reading: Helix Books, 1995) for systems; Air Combat Command White Paper, *Effects-Based Operations* (May 2002) for EBO; Joseph Strange, *Centers of Gravity & Critical Vulnerabilities: Building on the Clausewitizian Foundation So That We Can All Speak the Same Language,* (Quantico: Marine Corps University Foundation, 1996) and MCDP 1, *Warfighting* (20 June 1997) for COG and CV; and Gordon Wells, AUSA Landpower Essay No. 01-1,

The Joint Campaign Planning Model

The joint campaign planning model resides in chapter II "Campaign Plan Design" of JP 5-00.1, *Joint Doctrine for Campaign Planning.* The design is conducted in three steps classified as "the key elements of operational design" which are: "(1) understanding the strategic guidance…; (2) identifying the critical factors …; and (3) developing an operational concept or scheme that will achieve the strategic objective(s)."[50]

During the "understanding the strategic guidance" portion, the operational planner determines what must be accomplished and what conditions must be set to achieve the strategic goals. The strategic guidance provides the overarching framework by providing information on the strategic end state, resources, restraints, constraints and assumptions. The strategic guidance allows interagency integration through a focus on a commonly understood strategic end state. Additionally during this portion, termination criteria must be determined and subsequently integrated into future planning.

The "identifying critical factors" portion translates directly to the USMC operational concept of determining COGs and CVs. The joint doctrine promulgates almost exactly the Center of Gravity-Critical Capabilities-Critical Requirement-Critical Vulnerability analytical construct articulated by the Marine Corps University's Dr Joe Strange in *Centers of Gravity & Critical Vulnerabilities: Building on the Clausewitizian Foundation So That We Can All Speak the Same Language.* Understanding the definitions of the four terms of the analytical construct is crucial. COGs were defined above. Critical capabilities are the enablers, which allow the functioning of the COG and are necessary to accomplish objectives[51] "Critical requirements are those essential conditions, resources, and means for a critical capability to be fully operational."[52] The only difference between Dr Strange's construct and joint doctrine lies in the definition of

---

"The Center of Gravity Fad: Consequence of the Absence of an Overarching American Theory of War," (March 2001) for integrated campaign.

[50] Joint Publication 5-00.1, II-1.

[51] Ibid., II-7.

[52] Ibid., II-7.

critical vulnerability. Joint doctrine defines it as "those aspects or components of the...critical capabilities...which are deficient, or vulnerable to neutralization, interdiction or attack in a manner achieving decisive or significant results, disproportionate to the military resources applied," while Dr Strange states CV are critical requirements or their components.[53] Also essential during this portion of operational design is the achievement of an understanding of the operational environment. This allows COGs to be visualized "in terms of a system" and subsequently be subjected to detailed systemic analysis.[54] A systems approach should lead to focus and purpose in planning while also providing an understanding of operational protection requirements.

The last stage of the joint operational design process is to develop the operational concept. The concept provides a visualization of what will be done, how it will be done, the resources that will be used and the level of risk that is acceptable, all residing under the rubric of the strategic goal. The facets of operational art are applied in order to provide a visualization of the "campaign in terms of forces and functions involved."[55] The concept, at a minimum, details the defeat mechanism (often using decisive points and lines of operation), "application of forces and capabilities, sequencing, synchronization and integration of forces and capabilities and operational functions."[56]

Counterinsurgency

A frightening contradiction dominates the counterinsurgent environment: there is little indication that US skill in this type of conflict has grown as rapidly as the strategic relevance of insurgency.
-Steven Metz[57]

This section will describe the shortfalls in operational level planning for COIN through examination of historical and current thought and doctrine on COIN.

---

[53] Ibid., II-7 and Strange, 43.
[54] Ibid., II-8.
[55] Ibid., II-12.
[56] Ibid.
[57] Steven Metz, "Counterinsurgent Campaign Planning," *Parameters* 19, no. 3, (September 1989): 60.

Counterinsurgency Theory and Literature

COIN theory is generally categorized in terms of the colonial powers of the twentieth century, Britain, France, the United States and Russia (both Imperial and Soviet), due to a general consistency of thought and approach followed by these nations during counterinsurgent activities. Each nation's theory, general practice and literature will be briefly examined.

Britain conducted more counterinsurgencies and for longer periods of time than any of the other three nations, primarily due to her preeminence as the imperial power. Colonel Charles Callwell published one of the earliest works on COIN in 1896, *Small Wars: Their Principles and Practice*. Callwell's classic primarily deals with tactics, techniques and procedures, but its initial chapters do discuss operational issues such as the objective and the effect of logistics on the conduct of planning.[58] Between the World Wars, Charles Gwynn published *Imperial Policing*, which became the basis of British COIN doctrine, though it failed to recognize the emerging political nature of insurgency.[59] He provided four principles: civil primacy over the military, minimal use of military force, the need for firm and timely action and civil and military coordination and cooperation.[60] Post World War II, several British theorists and practioners emerged, most notably Robert Thompson, Julian Paget and Frank Kitson. Thompson published *Defeating Communist Insurgency: Experiences from Malaya and Vietnam*[61] in 1966, Paget published *Counter-Insurgency Operations: Techniques of Guerilla Warfare*[62] and Kitson published *Low Intensity Operations: Subversion, Insurgency and Peacekeeping*[63] in 1971. All

---

[58] Charles E Callwell, *Small Wars: Their Principles and Practice,* 3d ed. (London: His Majesty's Stationary Office; reprint, Lincoln: University of Nebraska Press, 1996).

[59] Ian F.W.Beckett, ed., *The Roots of Counter-Insurgency: Armies and Guerilla Warfare, 1900-1945,* (London: Blanford Press, 1988), 12.

[60] Leroy Thompson, *The Counterinsurgency Manual,* (London: Greenhill Books, 2002), 17. Also see

[61] Robert Thompson, *Defeating Communist Insurgency: Experiences from Malaya and Vietnam,* Studies in International Security: 10, (London: MacMillan Press, Ltd., 1966).

[62] Julian Paget, *Counter-Insurgency Operations: Techniques of Guerrilla Warfare,* (New York: Walker and Company, 1967).

[63] Frank Kitson, *Low Intensity Operations: Subversion, Insurgency, Peace-keeping,* (Harrisburg: Stackpole Books, 1971).

three are similar in basic concept with Thompson providing five principles for the conduct of

COIN, as follows:

(1) The government must have a clear political aim: to establish and maintain a free, independent and united country that is politically and economically stable and viable.
(2) The government must function in accordance with law.
(3) The government must have an overall plan.
(4) The government must give priority to defeating political subversion, not the guerillas.
(5) In the guerilla phase of an insurgency, a government must secure its base areas first.[64]

Paget and Kitson, both serving British Army officers at the time of their books' publications, applied more emphasis on intelligence and training of military forces, with Kitson advocating early control of a centralized intelligence apparatus by the military in COIN situations. As such, British COIN is viewed primarily as a social action with the recognition of genuine grievances by the insurgent forces specific to their situation.[65] John Shy and Thomas Collier categorize the British approach to COIN as "their colonial tradition at its best: tight integration of civil and military authority, minimum force with police instead of army used when possible, good intelligence…, administrative tidiness…, and a general readiness to negotiate for something less than total victory."[66]

The French also have an extensive history of COIN, primarily in North Africa and Indochina. The French are credited with the formulation and articulation of pacification as a COIN strategy. Joseph-Simon Galliéni developed and implemented the *taiche d'huile* (oil stain) method, now referred to as pacification, while serving in Tonkin in the early 1890s.[67] Post World War II, as the French struggled to reestablish and maintain their colonial empire, the doctrine of *guerre révolutionnaire* (revolutionary war) emerged. Colonel Roger Trinquier is considered one of the architects of *guerre révolutionnaire,* which he described in *La Guerre Moderne* (Modern War), published in 1961. Conceptually, *guerre révolutionnaire* was the articulation of the

---

[64] Robert Thompson, 50-57.

[65] Thomas E Miller, *The Efficacy of Urban Insurgency in the Modern Era* (Fort Leavenworth, KS: U.S. Army Command and General Staff College, 31 May 2002), 27.

[66] John Shy and Thomas W. Collier, 854.

20

perceived ongoing and continuous death struggle between free society and monolithic communism. Trinquier touched upon these ideas when he said, "In seeking a solution it is essential to realize that in modern warfare we are not up against just a few armed bands spread across a given territory, but rather against an *armed clandestine organization* whose essential role is to impose its will upon the population. Victory will be obtained only through the complete destruction of the organization. This is the master concept that must guide us in our study of modern warfare."[68] Significantly, *guerre révolutionnaire* attempted to be the flip side of Maoist insurgency doctrine, recognizing that control of the population is the key. However, its focus was on the ends and not the means, in practice disregarding the rule of law and restricting civil liberties, to include sanctioned torture, which led to its ultimate repudiation by its democratic society despite its tactical efficacy. Policy options allowed French decision makers were also significantly reduced due to its ideological nature requiring the complete destruction of insurgency.

American COIN doctrine, correctly or not, is largely identified with its failure in Vietnam. This is not entirely accurate. The US Army had extensive COIN experiences prior to World War I, notably in Cuba and in the Philippines, and during the Indian campaigns. The US Marine Corps had extensive experience between the wars in the Caribbean, leading to the formal publication of the *Small Wars Manual* in 1940. Smaller COIN efforts were conducted primarily by the Army in the Philippines and Greece after World War II. Thus, the failure in Vietnam is surprising based on the previous US COIN experiences. A significant work providing histories of most post World War II U.S. counterinsurgencies and addressing the failure in Vietnam is Douglas Blaufarb's *The Counterinsurgency Era: U.S. Doctrine and Performance*, published in

---

[67] Francis Toase, "The French Experience," in *The Roots of Counter-Insurgency: Armies and Guerilla Warfare, 1900-1945*, ed. Ian F.W. Beckett, (London: Blanford Press, 1988), 44.
[68] Roger Trinquier, *Modern Warfare: A French View of Counterinsurgency*, trans. by Daniel Lee (New York: Frederick A. Praeger, 1964), 8-9.

1977. Blaufarb's overall conclusion is the failure to recognize the limits of US power due to a failure to understand the US system, as well as the environment in which it is to be exercised.[69]

In 1984, in response to American failure in Vietnam and attempts to improve future conduct of COIN, Vice Chief of Staff of the Army, Maxwell Thurman, instituted empirical testing of insurgencies that could evaluate competing theories, predict outcomes and generate a new paradigm for future successes.[70] What emerged from this testing was a statistically significant model known as the U.S. Southern Command Small Wars Operations Research Directorate (SWORD) model or more commonly, the Manwaring Paradigm. The Manwaring Paradigm identified the six most salient variables in determining the success or failure of a COIN (or conversely an insurgency). They are as follows:

1) Legitimacy.
2) Organization.
3) Military and Other Support to a Targeted Government.
4) Intelligence
5) Discipline and Capabilities of the Armed Forces.
6) Reduction of Outside Aid to Insurgents.[71]

Significantly, the Manwaring Paradigm identified these as strategic variables. They still require translation through the operational level to tactical execution.

Larry Cable offers a different COIN concept where he postulates there are only two tools for the insurgent and the counterinsurgent: "popular perceptions of legitimacy and a credible capacity to coerce."[72] The art in COIN and the key to success, in Cable's view, lie in first understanding the tools individually, then their interactions with each other, and finally their

---

[69] Douglas S. Blaufarb, *The Counterinsurgency Era: U.S. Doctrine and Performance* (New York: The Free Press, 1977), 311. Also significant, despite his personal discreditment, is Larry Cable, *Conflict of Myths: The Development of American Counterinsurgency Doctrine and the Vietnam War,* (New York: New York University Press, 1986).

[70] Max G. Manwaring, *Internal Wars: Rethinking Problem and Response,* (Carlisle Barracks: Strategic Studies Institute, U.S. Army War College, September 2001), 17.

[71] Max G. Manwaring, "Toward an Understanding of Insurgency Wars: The Paradigm," in *Uncomfortable Wars: Toward a New Paradigm of Low Intensity Conflict,* ed. Max G. Manwaring, Westview Studies in Regional Security, ed. Wm. J. Olson (Boulder: Westview Press, 1991), 20-24.

[72] Larry Cable, "Reinventing the Round Wheel: Insurgency, Counter-Insurgency, and Peacekeeping Post Cold War," *Small Wars and Insurgencies* 4, no. 2 (Autumn 1993): 229.

application based on a specific operating environment and situation. Cable's model provides a systems view toward the planning and conduct of COIN.

Beginning in the late 1980s, an active, primarily academic, discussion began on the US Army's concept of Low Intensity Conflict (LIC), spawned largely by the conflicts in Central America. COIN was subsumed under the greater rubric of LIC, but was still a key component. The discussion largely broke down into two camps: the "war is war" view and the "Internal Defense and Development" view. The "war is war" camp considered LIC as an act of force to compel the enemy to do our will.[73] The "Internal Defense and Development" camp viewed COIN as primarily a political and informational struggle with the military playing a significant, but secondary, role. This discussion continues today, primarily within the military, as we deal with the current War on Terrorism.

A new and interesting aspect of American COIN is viewing insurgency as a complex adaptive system. Dr Thomas Marks postulates the formation of insurgencies is not an inevitable phenomenon. Instead, "insurgent movements involve a continuous process whereby leadership and followers establish links and interact with each other."[74] As in any complex system, the role of the environment is significant in how it affects leadership and followers. Additionally, there is an element of constant cognitive tension which must remain in order to maintain the goals of the insurgency rather than seeking solutions to immediate problems.[75]

The Russians also have a long and storied history of COIN. Mikhail Tukhachevsky, one of the formulators of Soviet operational and mechanized warfare doctrine, is, surprisingly, the "father of Soviet counterinsurgency" as well.[76] He had extensive COIN experience during the Russian civil war and against the Basmachis in Central Asia. In 1926, he published an article in

---

[73] Harry G. Summers, Jr, "A War Is a War Is a War Is a War," in *Low-Intensity Conflict: The Pattern of Warfare in the Modern World,* ed. Loren B. Thompson, (Lexington: Lexington Books, 1989), 27.
[74] Thomas A Marks, "Evaluating Insurgent/Counterinsurgent Performance," *Small Wars and Insurgencies* 11, no. 3 (Winter 2000): 33.
[75] Ibid., 34.

Voina I Revoliustiia (War and Revolution) called "Borba s Konterrevoliutsionnim Vosstaniam" (Struggle with counterrevolutionary uprisings). This provided a conceptual basis for Soviet COIN doctrine.[77] Tukhachevsky expressed a mature understanding of political and cultural factors in COIN, as well as the use of the full range of military, political and economic measures in response. However, he viewed political concessions as merely temporary until the end of the crisis and also advocated the use of collective punishment and mass deportation, a common practice in Soviet COIN.

US Counterinsurgency Doctrine

From 1973 forward, as promulgated in the Nixon Doctrine, the US armed forces no longer conducted COIN as a mission, but only provided support to others' counterinsurgencies. COIN is no longer a separate topic in the doctrinal publications of the US armed forces.[78] COIN has been amalgamated with other "nonconventional" military tasks, generally categorized as military operations other than war. Even still, COIN is often not addressed under its own subheading, falling under another set of covering terms ranging from nation assistance, internal defense and development (IDAD) and foreign internal defense. In large part, this bias is in response to the failure of the US COIN effort in South Vietnam.

Current COIN doctrine begins with Internal Defense and Development (IDAD) strategy. The IDAD strategy is the plan, developed by the host nation (HN) facing the insurgency, and assisted by the United States government. A HN's IDAD plan brings together all the elements of national power to create a coherent strategic whole by integrating civilian and military programs to counter the insurgents. Any IDAD strategy should manifest four functions: balanced

---

[76] Anthony James Joes, *Guerilla Warfare: A Historical, Biographical and Bibliographical Sourcebook,* (Westport: Greenwood Press, 1996), 188.

[77] Ian F.W. Beckett, *Encyclopedia of Guerilla Warfare,* (New York: Checkmark Books, 2001), 240.

[78] In fact, the Marine Corps FMFM 8-20 *Counterinsurgency* has never officially been superceded or redesignated from a Fleet Marine Field Manual to the current Marine Corps Doctrinal Publication (MCDP). It is no longer available from the Marine Corps Doctrine website.

development, security, neutralization and mobilization.[79] These four functions provide the ends, interpreted through the specific needs of the country, which the campaign plan will be designed to achieve. Significantly, the Department of State has the lead role in assisting the HN in developing its IDAD/counterinsurgency plan. (See Appendix B, a graphical representation of the IDAD model).

Foreign internal defense (FID) is the series of programs conducted by the US government involving all elements of national power and focused to support a HN's IDAD strategy.[80] FID is viewed primarily as a preventive measure and only used to counter a threat as a last resort. US FID policy is transmitted through National Security Council directives and distilled through Joint Strategic Planning System documents to the Geographic Combatant Commanders, who are responsible for FID planning within their areas of responsibility.

Geographic combatant commanders and their staffs (ideally) use the deliberate planning process in the Joint Operation Planning and Execution System to develop a FID program. They are guided by the FID basic planning imperatives: 1) consider long term or strategic effects of all US assistance efforts, 2) FID programs must be tailored to the specific environment and needs of the HN and, 3) the ultimate responsibility for IDAD rests with the HN.[81]

There are a number of issues that directly point to an operational shortfall in COIN doctrine. The first is the underlying assumption behind the concept of IDAD. The HN ruling authority must have the capability and the will to reform or transform itself, which inevitably transforms the political and economic dynamics of the HN society. Second, while IDAD strategy will still be appropriate in some cases, it has not changed to meet the challenges of the new transnational security environment nor emergent insurgency forms. Third, the IDAD doctrine was developed in the 1960s and has been passed forward virtually unchanged. The assimilation

---

[79] Joint Publication 3-07.1, *Joint Tactics, Techniques, and Procedures (JTTP) for Foreign Internal Defense (FID)*, 26 June 1996, C-1.
[80] Ibid., vii.
[81] Ibid., III-1.

of operational art by the US Army and systems theory by the joint community has not yet been applied to COIN. In this regard, Colonel James Greer, current director of the School for Advanced Military Studies states, "Today's doctrinal concepts for operational design hamstring planners' and commanders' abilities to design and conduct effective, coherent campaigns for operations across the spectrum of conflict in today's security environment."[82] Max Manwaring feels center of gravity needs to be "reconsidered and redefined for intrastate conflict."[83] Additionally, the IDAD concept, steeped in the bipolar world it was created in, calls for outright victory by the ruling authorities. Reconsideration of compromise, victory, and strategic advantage is required and should be viewed in terms of US national interests through the lens of the new security environment.

Finally, IDAD and FID require the orchestration of all elements of national power through full interagency and multinational integration in planning and execution. Again, Manwaring states "there is a critical requirement to teach people how to put a campaign plan together using a combination of civil and military resources to achieve a single comprehensive political aim."[84] In terms of coordination and cooperation, there is a planning and execution disconnect caused by the difference in scope visualized by the primary planners of FID and IDAD. Geographic Combatant Commanders, primarily responsible for FID, have a regional focus which then may extend down to a specific country. However, the ambassador and his country team have the responsibility for IDAD, which should drive FID planning and execution, but rarely raises visualization above a country focus.

Conclusion

This chapter addressed the theoretical and doctrinal foundations of operational art, campaign planning, and COIN. The appreciation of operational art occurred in the US military in the 1980s and a joint campaign planning model was not promulgated until 2002. US COIN

---

[82] Greer, 23.
[83] Max G. Manwaring, *Internal Wars: Rethinking Problem and Response*, 31.

doctrine was primarily written in the 1960s and has remained virtually unchanged in the past 40 years. Operational shortfalls exist in current COIN planning doctrine and practice. The following two case studies, the Philippines and El Salvador, will provide a vehicle with which to determine if the operational shortfalls in COIN planning can be bridged through application of the joint campaign planning model.

THE HUKBALAHAP IN THE PHILIPPINES

They tell me the Huks are socialistic, that they are revolutionary, but I haven't got the heart to go after them. If I worked in those sugar fields I'd probably be a Huk myself.
-General of the Army Douglas MacArthur[85]

Background

This section presents the demographic, geographic and historical (both general and insurgency specific) perspective to frame the conduct of the insurgency and COIN in the Philippines from 1946 through 1955. The case study itself is an exemplar in the conduct of COIN and offers valuable insights into the nature of campaign planning for COIN.

Demographic and Geographic Overview of the Philippines

The Philippine Islands are an archipelago of over 7,000 islands extending some 1,850 kilometers north to south. The total land area is roughly 300,000 square kilometers, roughly the size of Arizona, of which Luzon and Mindanao, the two largest islands, represent roughly 65 percent. The Philippines are east of Vietnam and northeast of Malaysia. The official languages are English and Pilipino, which is a variant of Tagalog. Roughly 85 percent of the population is Roman Catholic, but with a large Islamic population in the southern islands. The Philippines had a population of roughly 20 million in 1950. Malay, Spanish, Chinese, Negrito and American

---

[84] Ibid., 32.
[85] William Manchester, *American Caesar: Douglas MacArthur 1880-1964*, (Boston: Little, Brown and Company, 1978), 420.

form the basic ethnic/racial mix in the Philippines. Sources of unrest have traditionally been along socio-economic and religious lines versus racial.[86]

Historic Perspective

The Spanish, after Magellan discovered the Philippines in 1521, established a permanent settlement there in 1565. Six years later the colonial capital was established at Manila on Luzon. Manila, due to its deep water anchorage, proximity to ready food stocks and large population, became the center of political, military, economic, religious and cultural activity for the Philippines, a position it holds to this day. The purpose of the Spanish colonization of the Philippines was the exploitation of natural resources and the Christianization of the native population. The Spanish instituted individual land ownership replacing the native communal land use. The Spanish also introduced a number of cash crops for export, primarily tobacco and sugar. Both of these crops encouraged large plantations with a landlord-tenant system that became a constant source of friction and unrest in Filipino society.

There was a history of conflict between the Filipinos and the Spanish. Significant outbursts of revolt and political violence occurred between 1744 and 1872.[87] The last three decades of the 19th century saw the rise of Filipino nationalism, in large part inspired by the writings of José Rizal and the Propaganda Movement.[88] The 1890s saw a split between the Filipino upper class, who wanted reform through compromise with the Spanish government, and the people, who wanted independence, at the cost of revolution if necessary. This split saw the formation of the *Kaptipunan*, a religious secret society whose purpose was to gain Filipino

---

[86] Frederica M. Bunge, *Philippines: A Country Study,* (Washington, DC: U.S. Government Printings Office, DA PAM 550-72, 1984), xiv; Central Intelligence Agency, "Philippines" in *The World Factbook 2002,* 1 January 2002. Site at http://www.cia.gov/cia/publications/factbook/geos/es.html, accessed on 17 February 2003.
[87] Bunge, 14-17.
[88] Ibid., 18.

independence. The Filipinos revolted against the Spanish in 1896.[89] This insurgency was ongoing at the beginning of the Spanish American War.

In 1898, the United States invaded the Philippines as part of their war against Spain. Following the Spanish defeat by the US, the Filipinos, led by Emilio Aguinaldo, declared independence on 12 June 1898.[90] The Treaty of Paris, which ended the Spanish American War, ceded the Philippines to the US. By February 1899, the Filipinos were in revolt against the US in order to win their independence. The revolt was not subdued until 1903.

Following suppression of the Filipino insurgency, the US indicated the Philippines would not be a permanent colony. For the next three decades, the American administrators of the Philippines followed the general policy of preparing the Filipinos for independence. Rapid political development occurred during this period beginning with the election and convening of the popularly elected Filipino lower house of Congress in 1907.[91] In 1934, the US Congress passed the Tydings-Duffie Act, creating the Philippine Commonwealth and promising full independence by 1946.[92]

Unfortunately, the US did little to reform the social and economic structure of the Philippines. Social unrest began to bubble forth as a result of a rapidly growing population and decay in the traditional benefits the *patron* provided laborers under the landlord-tenant system. Internal distribution of wealth continued to become more unbalanced and led to the establishment of peasant worker societies and a greater participation in other radical political organizations.

The Philippines Communist Party and the Huks

The 1920s saw the introduction of communism and socialism to the Philippines, primarily in Central Luzon in response to labor struggles. Pedro Abad Santos formed the

---

[89] Ibid., 21.
[90] Ibid., 23.
[91] Ibid., 27.
[92] Clarence G. Barrens, "I Promise: Magsaysay's Unique PSYOP 'Defeats' Huks," Masters Thesis, (U.S. Army Command and General Staff College, 1970), 25.

Socialist Party of the Philippines in 1929.[93] Crisanto Evangelista, a well respected labor organizer, formed the *Partido Komunista ng Pilipinas* (The Philippine Communist party, PKP) in 1930.[94] In 1931, the PKP was outlawed. Jacinto Manahan, another early PKP member, broke from the party and formed the *Kalipunang Pambansa ng mga Magsasaka sa Pilipinas* (National Society of Peasants in the Philippines, KPMP) in 1931.[95] In 1932, Luis Taruc, organized the *Aguman ding Maldang Talapaobra* (General Workers' Union, AMT), and in October 1935 became the general secretary of the Socialist Party.[96] The Socialist Party and the PKP merged in 1938, maintaining the name of the PKP.[97]

As war with Japan approached in 1941, the PKP approached the Commonwealth government to offer their services in the fight.[98] Their offer was refused, but the PKP urged all "anti-Fascist" organizations, like the KPMP, AMT and labor unions, to prepare for guerilla warfare against the Japanese.[99] Following the Japanese invasion, the AMT and KPMP were placed under the operational control of the PKP.[100]

On 29 March 1942, the *Hukbo ng Bayan laban sa Hapon* (The People's Anti-Japanese Army, Huk), or shortened to the Tagalog acronym, Hukbalahap was formed as the military arm of the PKP.[101] Initially, the majority of the force came from the KPMP.[102] Luis Turac became the supreme commander (*El Supremo*) of Huk forces and Casto Alejandrino became his deputy.

The Huks organized action units of 100 men, which they termed squadrons. Two or more squadrons formed a battalion, and two or more battalions a regiment. Five military districts were formed to control geographic areas of responsibility, and were assigned regiments. In

---

[93] , Eduardo Lachica, *The Huks: Philippine Agrarian Society in Revolt,* (New York: Praeger Publishers, 1971), 82.
[94] Ibid., 97.
[95] Ibid., 100.
[96] Ibid., 89.
[97] Ibid., 101.
[98] Greenberg, 12.
[99] Lachica, 103.
[100] Greenberg, 14.
[101] Ibid., 15.

addition to their field forces, the Huks created Barrio United Defense Corps (BUDC), which

acted as local shadow governments and the Huk infrastructure. Additionally, the Huks

established a "struggle force," which was primarily a logistics acquisition and distribution force,

and a Department of Culture and Information, which provided political advisors to the squadron

and BUDCs.[103]

The Huks served with distinction as a guerilla force in the Philippines during World War

II. By the time of the liberation of Manila in February 1945, the Huks had conducted 1,200

combat actions and killed 25,000 Japanese or Filipino collaborators, and fielded 15,000 guerillas

with an infrastructure of at least 100,000. [104] However, during the conduct of the war the Huks

operated independently from the United States Armed Forces Far East (USAFFE) sponsored

guerilas, and received minimal supplies through US channels. Due to US' distrust of the Huks'

political motives, attempts were made to rapidly disarm Huk units soon after areas were liberated.

Additionally, unlike USAFFE guerilla units, most Huk units were not recognized as fighting

forces and subsequently were not recognized or compensated for their wartime service, nor

integrated into the new Philippine Military Police Command.[105] At the end of the war, Taruc and

Alejandrino were arrested and detained for seven months by the US Counter Intelligence Corps.

This action, in conjunction with the failure to recognize Huk wartime service, created bitterness

toward the US and resparked a belief by the Huks that social justice could only be obtained

through armed struggle.[106]

With the end of the war, the PKP formed a political front called the Democratic Alliance

(DA). Additionally, it formed a new peasant agrarian organization, *Pambansang Kaisahan ng*

---

[102] Benedict J. Kerkvliet, *The Huk Rebellion: A Study of Peasant Revolt in the Philippines,* (Berkeley: University of California Press, 1977. Reprint, Lanham: Rowman & Littlefield Publishers, Inc, 2002), 67.
[103] Kerkvliet, 94-95; Greenberg, 20, 27; Richard H. Sanger, *Insurgent Era: New Patterns of Political, Economic, and Social Revolution* (Washington, DC: Potomac Books, Inc., 1967), 131.
[104] Kenneth Hammer, "Huks in the Philippines," *Military Review* 36, no. 1, (April 1956): 51.
[105] Ibid., 52. Greenberg, 33. Only two Huk squadrons were recognized and paid and their AOR had been southern Luzon.
[106] Thomas A. Grant, "Little Wars, Big Problems: The United States and Counterinsurgency in the Postwar World," Ph.D. diss., (University of California, Irving, 1990), 146.

mga Magbubukid (National Peasants Union, PKM) by combining the AMT and the KPMP.[107]

Taruc and Alejandrino became congressional candidates for the DA and were elected to congress

with four other DA candidates in 1946. The DA candidates were unseated through a measure

passed by the Liberals, the majority party, a political move that fueled unrest in central Luzon.

On 24 August 1946, Juan Feleo, a DA spokesman, and a number of other peasant leaders were

assassinated by unidentified uniformed men.[108] This was the last straw for the Huks and violence

erupted.

Ramon Magsaysay

Ramon Magsaysay was born in 1907, the son of a schoolteacher. Magsaysay put himself

through college working as a mechanic for a bus company and later worked his way up to

manage the regional operations of the company. After the Japanese attacks on Pearl Harbor and

the Philippines, Magsaysay joined the army, was commissioned as a captain and assigned to run

transportation for the 31st US Division. In April 1942, Magsaysay linked up with COL (USA)

Gyles Merrill in Magsaysay's home province of Zambales to help form a USAFFE sponsored

guerilla resistance organization. Magsaysay originally served as the supply officer.[109] He later

became the commander of the unit and at the war's end had command of roughly 12,000 men.

His success as a tactical commander led the Japanese to place a one million Philippine peso price

on his head.[110] At the recommendation of COL Merrill, GEN MacArthur appointed Magsaysay

as the military governor of Zambales province in February 1945. At the request of his soldiers

and the future Filipino president, Magasaysay ran for and won the congressional seat for

Zambales in 1946. As a congressman, he served as the chairman of the House Armed Services

Committee until September 1950, when he was appointed the Secretary of National Defense to

fight the Huk insurgency.

---

[107] Lachica, 119.
[108] Ibid., 121.
[109] Carlos P. Romulo and Marvin D. Gray, *The Magsaysay Story,* (New York: The John Day Company, 1956), 45-46.

The Conduct of Insurgency and Counterinsurgency in the Phillipines

> When the war ended, the Party leaders said that only under unbearable provocation from the reactionary elements would the Huks take up arms again, in self-defense.
>
> -Luis Taruc[111]

> Gentlemen, I know you all have graduated from military establishments here and in the United States. Now I am telling you to forget everything you were taught at Ft. Leavenworth, Ft. Benning, and the Academy. The Huks are fighting an unorthodox war. We are going to combat them in unorthodox ways. Whatever it was that hurt me most as a guerilla is what we are now going to do to the Huk.
>
> -Ramon Magsaysay[112]

The Philippine insurgency and COIN falls into two distinct periods. The initial period runs from 1946 to late 1950. The period is marked by the near total collapse of the Philippine government. The transition from the first to the second phase is difficult to pinpoint exactly, but is generally considered 1 September 1950, the date Ramon Magsaysay was appointed as the Secretary of National Defense. Concurrently with the appointment of Magsaysay, the US government began to focus attention on the deteriorating economic, military and political situation in the Philippines. The second phase is characterized by Philippine government's seizure of the initiative and the destruction of the Huk insurgency as a social and military threat.

First Phase: Imminent Collapse

President Manuel Roxas, the first president of the Republic of the Philippines, pledged to end the Huk insurgency in sixty days after his inauguration through the policy called the "mailed fist." In fact, Roxas viewed the Huks as people conducting criminal acts, not as organized insurgents.[113] He failed. The Military Police Command (MPC) rarely inflicted damage on the Huks, and their poor results and abuse of civilians reduced the legitimacy of the government.

---

[110] Greenberg , 80.

[111] Luis Taruc, *He Who Rides the Tiger: The Story of an Asian Guerilla Leader* (New York: Frederick A. Praeger, Publishers, 1967), 24.

[112] Greenberg, 87; Romulo and Gray, 112.,

[113] Dana R. Dillon, "Comparative Counter-insurgency Strategies in the Phillipines," *Small Wars and Insurgencies* 6, no. 3 (Winter 1995): 283.

From 1946 to 1948, the Huks conducted numerous hit and run raids, and controlled territory in central Luzon, known as Huklandia. The government staged a large offensive action in the vicinity of Mount Arayat, the Huk heartland, in early 1947, without much effect. In 1948, President Roxas declared the Huks and the PKM illegal organizations, and reinstated the "mailed fist" policy. Roxas died in April 1948, and was replaced by vice-president Elpido Quirino.

Quirino initially tried an amnesty policy leading to a truce and negotiations with the Huks. Taruc was allowed to take his elected position in congress. However, the Huks were negotiating from a position of strength relative to the government and used the truce period to consolidate their territorial control, gather strength, rest and rearm. After four months the truce broke down, and Taruc resumed command of the Huk forces. In 1948, the Huks also changed their name to *Hukbong Magapalaya ng Bayan* (The People's Liberation Army, HMB), and began an offensive that ran from November 1948 to April 1949.[114]

The general and presidential election was held in 1949. President Quirino won the presidential election; however, the election was rife with political violence and vote fraud. The majority of the Filipino electorate no longer accepted that societal reform was possible through the democratic process.[115] The Huks exploited this disillusionment with a major information effort under the slogan, "Bullets not ballots." The Huks also increased military attacks, beginning to transition from guerilla to mobile warfare, occupying towns and directly assaulting constabulary stations.[116]

In addition to the electoral crisis, the Filipino government also faced a financial crisis, primarily caused by corruption and inefficiency. This reinforced the decline of public faith in the

---

[114] The offensive effectively ended with the assasination of Mrs Manuel Quezon, widow of nationalist Manuel Quezon, her daughter and the mayor of Quezon City. There was a national backlash against the Huks for this act of terrorism. The HMB high command declared that this was an unauthorized attack and publicly punished those involved.

[115] Sanger, 134. There were over 200 politically motivated deaths on election day alone.

[116] A.H.Peterson, G.C. Reinhard and E.E. Conger, eds., *Symposium on the Role of Airpower in Counterinsurgency and Unconventional Warfare: The Philippine Huk Campaign,* (Santa Monica: RAND, RM-3652-PR, July 1963), 15.

government. "By the end of 1949, the government seemed willing to let the military go unpaid and the education system to wither for want of funds, even to succumb to the Huk rebellion, rather than face up to the minimum responsibility for government function."[117]

In January 1950, the Huk Politburo declared a revolutionary situation existed in the Philippines, directing that a "geometric progression" in Huk membership be launched, and that the military strategy convert from guerilla operations to mobile warfare.[118] Attacks increased 1000 percent from their pre-1950 levels, and also increased in boldness.[119] The Chief of Staff of the Philippine Armed Forces was ambushed two miles from his headquarters in a Manila suburb.[120] In May, three major cities were overrun and held for several days. In August, some 500 Huks defeated an Army battalion in the field, and then overran their garrison, which had an army convalescent hospital.[121] By this time, the Huks had 15,000 armed insurgents and a mass support base of 2 million.[122] The Huks planned to seize Manila by the end of the year and have complete control over the Philippines by May 1952.[123]

Second Phase: Seizing the Initiative and Defeating the Huks

The large scale attacks and the precipitous decline of the government finally forced a realization on both the Quirino administration and the US government that drastic action must be taken to preserve a democratic Philippines. This manifested in actions taken to improve the overall government functionality and military effort. The Bell Trade Mission conducted an economic survey of the Philippines, releasing their report in October 1950. As a result of this

---

[117] Frank H. Golay, *The Philippines: Public Policy and National Economic Development,* Ithaca: Cornell University Press, 1961, 71-72; quoted in Dana R. Dillon, "Comparative Counter-insurgency Strategies in the Philippines," *Small Wars and Insurgencies* 6, no. 3, (Winter 1995), 285

[118] William Chapman, *Inside the Philippine Revolution,* (New York: W.W. Norton & Company, 1987), 63; Greenberg, 64. This was cause for serious disagreement between Luis Taruc and the PKP leaders, principally Jose and Jesus Lava. Taruc felt the time for mobile warfare had not come.

[119] Greenberg, 65.

[120] Sanger, 136; Peterson, 19. The Chief of Staff survived but his aide de camp was killed in the attack.

[121] Greenberg, 66; Peterson, 15; Edward G. Lansdale, *In the Midst of Wars: An American's Mission to Southeast Asia,* (New York: Harper & Row, Publishers, 1972. Reprint, New York: Fordham University Press, 1991), 26-29. Lansdale's account provides an insight of the utter disillusionment of the people with the government of the Philippines in 1950.

[122] Peterson, 17.

35

report, President Quirino signed an agreement with President Truman stating that sound financial

practices would be established and pursued. US economic aid was contingent on the execution of

this agreement.[124] In terms of the military effort, reorganization of the armed forces into battalion

combat teams (BCT) was undertaken and increased US military aid was pursued. Most

significantly, Congressman Ramon Magsaysay resigned his position as chair of the Armed

Services Committee to become the Secretary of National Defense, with virtually unlimited

authority provided by President Quirino to defeat the Huk insurgency.

Magsaysay immediately launched a COIN campaign using the slogan "All Out

Friendship or All Out Force."[125] Significant reform and reorganization of the Philippine military

began, greatly facilitated by US aid, known as the Army Attraction Program.[126] This program

included a massive increase in the size and capability of the army from ten to twenty six BCTs,

integration of tactical psychological operations, assumption of the Philippine Constabulary into

the armed forces, pay raises for soldiers, removal from the service of undesirable officers and

enlisted soldiers, systematic elimination of corruption and other unlawlessness, the return of an

offensive spirit through small unit action, improvement of collection and distribution of

intelligence, and expanded civic action programs. Additionally, other programs boosted the

legitimacy of the government or isolated the Huks from supplies and the population. A weapons

buy-back program resulted in the purchase of 15,000 weapons, 110,000 hand grenades and 14

million rounds of ammunition in less than four years.[127] The most famous of these programs was

the Economic Development Corps (EDCORPS), which provided government land, funds, and

farming equipment to surrendered Huks.

---

[123] Sanger, 136.
[124] Dana R. Dillon, "Comparative Counter-insurgency Strategies in the Philippines," *Small Wars and Insurgencies* 6, no. 3, (Winter 1995), 287.
[125] Napoleon D. Valeriano and Charles T.R. Bohannan, *Counter-Guerilla Operations: The Philippine Experience,* (New York: Frederick A. Praeger, Publisher, 1962), 103.
[126] Peterson, 18.
[127] Dillion, 290. This reduced Huk weapons stores by an estimated fifty percent.

Shortly after his appointment as Secretary of Defense, Magsaysay was instrumental in the capture of the Huk politburo in Manila 18 October 1950. The capture not only disrupted the command and control structure of the Huks, but was also instrumental in disrupting a Huk offensive planned for November 1950. Even more significantly, it was a major intelligence coup. Some five metric tons of documents were captured outlining plans and organizations, and providing names of Huk guerillas and supporters. Additionally, it led to a major policy change by the Philippine government, suspending the writ of *habeas corpus* for suspected insurgents until completion of the anti-Huk campaign.[128]

The November 1950 Huk Offensive, disrupted by the capture of the Manila Politburo, failed to capture of Manila. In January 1951, the Armed Forces of the Philippines (AFP) launched a two month offensive called OPERATION SABER, which struck the Huk base areas identified in the captured Politburo documents.[129] Throughout 1951, the government wrested the initiative from the Huk insurgents, and began to seriously interdict the Huk lines of communication. By the end of 1951, the AFP had increased by sixty percent toa strength of 53,700, with twenty six BCTs, and had gained valuable combat experience.[130]

The elections of 1951, in conjunction with the AFP's seizure of the initiative, were the turning point in the pursuit of governmental legitimacy. Magsaysay promised the nation a "clean" election and then delivered it. The military, to include the reserves, and ROTC cadets were used to protect polling sites. Political violence was drastically reduced. The result of the elections was a significant moral defeat for the Huks. Huk surrenders began to increase dramatically in December 1951.[131]

---

[128] Greenberg, 129. The significance of this policy change, conducted at this time, can not be overstated. First, the government acted at a time to make this suspension politically feasible, due to the positive press from the capture of the Politburo. Second, it significantly decreased the amount of human rights violations in the field since suspected guerillas could now be detained instead of "tactically" interrogated.
[129] Ibid., 130.
[130] Ibid., 131. The AFP provided a BCT to Korea on a rotating basis. Officers thought to be performing below their capabilities were threatened with transfer to duty with the BCT in Korea.
[131] Ibid., 133.

By early 1952, the Huks had been forced to return to guerilla operations. The AFP kept pressure on the Huks by mounting multiple extended large scale offensives and through constant small unit actions. Huk casualties rose significantly while AFP casualties fell.

In many ways, 1953 was a watershed year for the COIN. It saw the resignation of Magsaysay as Minister of Defense and his election and inauguration as President. It also saw continued exploitation of the military initiative by the AFP against the Huks. Magsaysay, in his letter of resignation to President Quirino, stated the need for more than military action against the Huks. He wrote, "Under your concept of my duties as Secretary of National Defense, my job is just to go on killing Huks. But you must realize that we cannot solve the problem of dissidence simply by military measures. It would be futile to go on killing Huks, while the administration continues to breed dissidence by neglecting the problems of our masses."[132] Following his resignation, Magsaysay announced his candidacy for president with the opposition party. Once again, the Army ensured the legality of the election and deterred significant political violence. Magsaysay won by an overwhelming margin, and became president in December of 1953.

With Magsaysay as president, 1954 saw the end of a Huk threat to the national government, though operations against scattered bands continued for several years more. In February 1954, the AFP launched OPERATION THUNDER-LIGHTENING in the vicinity of Mount Arayat, which involved over 5,000 troops and lasted approximately 7 months.[133] The result was the surrender of Luis Taruc on 17 May. Concurrently, the AFP launched other operations in areas with remaining Huk forces. The combined offensives effectively ended the military threat by the Huks. On the civil front, President Magsaysay began large scale infrastructure improvements and agrarian reform, and moved to eliminate corruption throughout the government. The combined effects of the complete government effort ended the Huk threat.

---

[132] Romulo and Gray, 193.
[133] Greenberg, 140.

The United States' Strategic Objectives for the Philippines

The US government had three basic policy goals for the Philippines from late 1950 onward as promulgated in NSC 84/2, "A Report to the President by the National Security Council on the Position of the United States with Respect to the Philippines."[134] NSC 84/2 stated, "The United States has as its objectives in the Philippines the establishment and maintenance of: a. An effective government which will preserve and strengthen the pro-U.S. orientation of the people. b. A Philippine military capability [sic] of restoring and maintaining internal security. c. A stable and self-supporting economy."[135] It went on to say,

> To accomplish the above objectives, the United States should:
> a. Persuade the Philippine government to effect political, financial, economic and agricultural reforms in order to improve the stability of the country.
> b. Provide such military guidance and assistance as may be deemed advisable by the United States and acceptable to the Philippine Government.
> c. Extend, under United States supervision and control, appropriate economic assistance in the degree corresponding to progress made toward creating the essential conditions of internal stability.
> d. Continue to assume responsibility for the external defense of the Islands and be prepared to commit United States forces, if necessary, to prevent communist control of the Philippines.[136]

The Campaign Plan in the Philippines

> Quirino studied the memorandum [of Magsaysay's plan to defeat the Huks] carefully. He looked up at Magsaysay and with an edge of some bewilderment in his voice, he said: "I have never heard of these tactics. General Castenada (the armed force chief of staff) has never suggested anything like this to me."
> *-The Magsaysay Story*[137]

There is no doubt that the Philippine government had no strategic plan to combat the insurgency prior to the appointment of Magsaysay as Secretary of Defense. Equally certain, Magsaysay developed an outline plan based on a strategic objective to combat the insurgency when he became the Secretary of Defense. The basis of his plan was recognition that defeating

---

[134] Daniel B. Schirmer and Stephen R. Shalom, ed, *The Philippines Reader: A History of Colonialism, Neocolonialism, Dictatorship and Resistance,* (Boston: South End Press, 1987), 105.

[135] U.S. National Security Council Staff, "A Report to the President by the National Security Council with Respect to the Philippines," NSC 84/2, 9 November 1950, in *The Philippines Reader: A History of Colonialism, Neocolonialism, Dictatorship and Resistance,* ed. Daniel B. Schirmer and Stephen R. Shalom, (Boston: South End Press, 1987), 110.

[136] Ibid.

[137] Romulo and Gray, 105.

the Huks was not a military problem at its most basic, but instead rested on the moral right to govern and the government's social contract with Philippine society. Magsaysay understood that the insurgency's underpinnings were based on legitimate grievances and that the insurgents themselves were not the enemy. Magsaysay's outline plan had as its overarching strategic objective restoration of governmental legitimacy, achieved through isolating the Huk insurgents from all aspects of Philippine society, using the unified and integrated application of the elements of national power, with the informational element being primary.

While Magsaysay had a strategic framework, he did not have a fully developed operational campaign plan. Understanding obtained in his tenure as chairman of the House Armed Services Committee allowed him to immediately begin reforming the military under the Army Attraction Program. This was still done under the rubric of his strategic framework and focused on the informational element. He directed that every soldier's primary mission was to be an ambassador to develop good will for his unit and the government, and that his secondary mission was to kill Huks.[138] He reinforced this concept constantly in his visits to units, by telling soldiers, "Your uniform is the symbol of our national sovereignty and you must treat it with respect and see that it is respected."[139] He instituted reforms and took actions that reinforced his mission statement to the soldiers, to include pay raises, the suspension of *habeus corpus*, removal of poor officers and NCOs, and increasing the capabilities of the armed forces through reorganization, expansion and training.

To address areas outside the immediate military reforms, he conducted a complete internal defense estimate, including the whole of national internal policy, prior to taking decisive action against the insurgency.[140] From this estimate, the campaign plan to combat the Huks was developed. It was at this point in 1950, that Edward Lansdale and the Joint US Military Aid Group (JUSMAG) made their critical contribution. The relationship of explicit and implicit trust

---

[138] Valeriano and Bohannan, 105.
[139] Romulo and Gray, 127.

40

developed between Lansdale and Magsaysay allowed Lansdale to become Magsaysay's *de facto* advisor. In this role, Lansdale's suggestions, particularly on the informational front, were incorporated into the operational plan within the strategic framework. A major contribution was the formation of the Civil Affairs Office (CAO), a psychological warfare division as part of the staff of the Secretary of Defense, whose members Lansdale largely personally trained.[141] Other contributions were the innovative use of aircraft in conducting psychological operations and the development of a number of psychological operations products supporting government themes.[142] Lansdale and the JUSMAG also provided critical intelligence and evaluation assistance, which facilitated the identification of adaptations and transitions in the base campaign plan. Finally, the JUSMAG provided critical financial aid and diplomatic pressure on the Philippine government to support the COIN campaign.

The COIN campaign focused on separating the insurgents from Philippine society, and included persuasive and coercive elements. Isolation of the insurgents from Philippine society was pursued across the spectrum, but always with the informational aspect to the forefront. Insurgent leadership and organization were targeted. Amnesty programs, especially EDCORPS, demonstrated the government's willingness to reintegrate insurgents into society. Insurgent logistics was targeted through a weapons buy-back program and focused interdiction of guerilla production bases. Insurgent morale and military capability were targeted through relentless offensive action by the AFP, robbing the Huks of security and sanctuary. Popular support was addressed through reform of the military, civic action programs, agrarian reform, psychological operations, judiciary reform and electoral reform. Transitions to greater levels of civic actions

---

[140] Barrens, 66; Campbell, 129.

[141] Lansdale, 70. The CAO was attached to BCTs and worked directly for the BCT commanders. However, they also reported directly to Magsaysay as members of his staff, acting as a "directed telescope" for him. Additionally, the members of the CAO were handpicked and in a secondary role acted as "political commissars" for Magsaysay ensuring execution of his policies, particularly the Army Attraction Program.

[142] Light aircraft were used to track Huk patrols and then broadcast PSYOPs messages to them via bullhorn. The most famous PSYOP product was "The Eye of God," an eye dropped in leaflet form or put near work areas or houses of known or suspected Huk supporters to indicate the government was watching them.

based on local security reinforced acceptance of governmental legitimacy. Most significantly, all government actions remained focused on the strategic objective.

Conclusion

The COIN effort in the Philippines was extremely successful. After the appointment of Magsaysay as Secretary of Defense, the government of the Philippines, with the assistance of the US government, focused its various efforts on defeating the Huk insurgency. Magsaysay developed a strategic outline, leading to the development of a flexible campaign plan, which unified and integrated the means of the Philippine government to defeat the Huks. Magsaysay's strategic focus on the moral right to govern facilitated addressing legitimate grievances and reintegration of the insurgents into Filipino society. Regrettably, due to his untimely death in 1957, many of the reforms he began were never institutionalized. The decline of social conditions in the Philippines gave rise to a new insurgency, the New People's Army, in 1969.

EL SALVADOR, 1981-1992

For the United States, on the other hand, El Salvador represents an experiment, an attempt to reverse the record of American failure in waging small wars, an effort to defeat an insurgency by providing training and material support without committing American troops to combat
-"The Four Colonel's Report"[143]

Recognizing the elements necessary for success, America has believed that it need merely find a catalyst to set them in motion.
-Benjamin C. Schwarz[144]

The official beginning of the civil war in El Salvador is often considered to be 10 January 1981, the launch of the Farabundo Martí National Liberation Front's (FMLN) first "Final Offensive." For the next eleven years, the United States would support the government of El Salvador's (GOES) COIN effort at a cost of 75,000 Salvadorans and 17 American officials

---

[143] A.J Bacevich and others, *American Policy in Small Wars: The Case of El Salvador* (Special Report), (Washington, D.C.:Pergamon-Brassey's, 1988), 1.
[144] Benjamin C. Schwarz, *American Counterinsurgency Doctrine and El Salvador: The Frustrations of Reform and the Illusions of Nation Building,* (Santa Monica: RAND, R-4042-USDP, 1991), 58.

deaths, and close to $6 billion in aid.[145] The war ended on 16 January 1992, when the insurgents

and the government signed a United Nations brokered permanentcease fire in Mexico City. The

US achieved strategic success, a democratically based government in El Salvador. However,

both the insurgents and the government claimed victory, based on a compromise solution that

allowed each to save face.

Background

This section presents the demographic, geographic and historical (both general and

insurgency specific) perspective to frame the conduct of the insurgency and COIN in El Salvador.

Demographic and Geographic Overview of El Salvador

El Salvador is the smallest of the Central American countries, smaller than the state of

Massachusetts, with roughly 20,720 square kilometers of land mass. Its small size and large

population make it the Central American nation with the highest population density. It has land

borders with Guatemala and Honduras, and shares a water boundary with Nicaragua in the Bay of

Fonseca. The country is primarily Spanish speaking, predominantly Roman Catholic. Politically,

it is subdivided into fourteen departments for local governance.[146]

Historical Perspective

From its colonization by Spain, El Salvador has seen cyclic economic crises, brought on

primarily by dependence on a single export crop (cacao, then indigo, and then coffee), which

have often led to popular revolts, repression and further consolidation of economic and political

power in the hands of the ruling elite. The most famous of these revolts, known as *La Matanza*

(the Massacre), occurred in February 1932, largely precipitated by plummeting coffee prices due

to the global depression of the 1930s. A communist-inspired revolt, it resulted in the deaths of

roughly 100 soldiers and civilians by the communists, and between 10,000 and 30,000 civilians

---

[145] Ibid., 2-3.
[146] Central Intelligence Agency, "El Salvador" in *The World Factbook 2002,* 1 January 2002, Site at http://www.cia.gov/cia/publications/factbook/geos/es.html. Accessed on 30 January 2003.

by the government in reprisal.[147] The Massacre is often cited as the root of the insurgency in the 1980s, in part because of the government's execution of Augustín Farabundo Martí, and in part because the military's assumption of political power immediately prior to the revolt. The army staged a *golpe* (coup d'etat) on December 2, 1931, and from then until the coup in 1979, the army exercised the direct political power of the state, despite the general pretense of legislative democracy and elections. El Salvador's oligarchy, known as the "Fourteen Families," supported this arrangement since the army protected their political, social and economic interests.

The 1960s saw continued economic strain, growing communist party agitation and the rise of a reformist opposition party, the Christian Democrats (PDC). The PDC grew rapidly and by 1968 began to challenge the army and "Fourteen Families". José Napoleón Duarte, who served as the mayor of San Salvador from 1964 to 1970, became the dominant public figure of the PDC. In 1969, El Salvador won the four day "Soccer War" with Honduras. The war had a significant negative economic impact on El Salvador's already ailing economy because it was expensive, forced great numbers of Salvadorans working in Honduras to return, and eliminated its previously primary market, Honduras.

In 1972, Duarte ran for president as a member of a combined opposition party on a platform of measured reform. He won, but was denied the position because of alleged vote fraud. After participating in a failed coup attempt, he was exiled to Venezuela. The 1970s gave rise to the leftist insurgent organizations that later formed the FMLN. A number of right wing paramilitary organizations also emerged that would come to be collectively known as the death squads.

The Road to Insurgency

In 1977, the Army stayed in power through vote fraud and repression, making Carlos Romero, former Minister of Defense, the president. His presidency began with the National

---

[147] John Waghelstein, *El Salvador: Observations and Experiences in Counterinsurgency,* (Carlisle Barracks: US Army War College, 1985), 4.

44

Police firing on a demonstration in support of the opposition candidate. Until his removal from office by coup on 15 October 1979, his tenure was marked by strikes and mass demonstrations, government repression, kidnappings by the left wing and assassinations by the right wing.

A junta of young, reform-minded army officers overthrew President Romero in October 1979, but dissolved in January 1980, to return immediately as a coalition between conservative military officers and the Christian Democrats. Duarte returned from exile to become president. In March 1980, Duarte and the junta presented a three phase program for agrarian reform and enacted the first phase. The same day, all banks and external commerce was nationalized and a state of siege was declared. However, these reforms were not enough to stem the downward spiral to full blown civil war. Political violence was rampant with an estimated 15,000 political deaths in 1980.[148] The economy continued to deteriorate with a 9 percent drop in Gross Domestic Product and unemployment rose to 17 percent.[149]

Following the Sandinista takeover of Nicaragua in the summer of 1979, Nicaragua and Cuba decided revolution in El Salvador required unity of effort among the El Salvadoran insurgent organizations. A meeting was sponsored by Cuba in Managua, Nicaragua, which brought together the five principal insurgent groups (the Salvadoran Communist Party, the Popular Liberation Front, the Popular Revolutionary Army, the National resistance and the Central American Workers Party).[150] The groups were promised military equipment, training and sanctuary, but only if they formed a unified opposition front. While serious animosities and ideological differences still abounded, the groups agreed to the terms to create a unified front. They formed a supreme executive body, known as the Unified Revolutionary Directive (DRU), a

---

[148] Hugh Byrne, *El Salvador's Civil War: A Study of Revolution,* (Boulder: Lynne Rienner Publishers, 1996), 81.
[149] Ibid., 74.
[150] José A.M. Bracamonte and David E. Spencer, *Strategy and Tactics of the Salvadoran FMLN Guerillas: Last Battle of the Cold War, Blueprint for Future Conflicts,* (Wesport: Praeger, 1995), 3-4.

45

political wing, known as the Democratic Revolutionary Front (FDR), and a military wing, known as the FMLN.[151]

The actions of the insurgents, as well as the extralegal activity by the right, deeply concerned the US government. Following the assassination of Catholic Archbishop Oscar Romero in 1980, President Jimmy Carter resumed "non-lethal" military aid, which had been suspended since 1977, as an attempt to use aid as the "stick" to affect GOES reform.[152] After four US churchwomen were tortured and killed in December 1980, the US immediately cut all aid to the GOES, but resumed economic aid two weeks later due to fear of the imminent collapse of the Salvadoran economy. The US resumed military aid after the start of the "Final Offensive" in January 1981.[153]

The Conduct of Insurgency and Counterinsurgency in El Salvador

Cuando la historia no se puede con la pluma, hay que escríbirla con el fusil(When history can no longer be written with the pen, it must be written with the rifle).
-Augustín Farabundo Martí[154]

Despite internal ideological differences, the FMLN decided on a primarily military based strategy to achieve victory over the GOES. On 10 January 1981, the FMLN launched its "Final Offensive" to produce a popular uprising and rapidly overthrow the GOES prior to the inauguration of Ronald Reagan in the US. The FLMN believed a communist government in El Salvador could be presented as a fait accompli to the incoming US president. After three weeks of hard fighting, the El Salvadoran Armed Forces (ESAF) managed to avert defeat and prevented the FMLN from achieving its strategic objectives. The ESAF was stretched to the breaking point and scattered throughout the country, however, which facilitated insurgent control of large areas of the country.

---

[151] Waghelstein, A-1.
[152] Robert B. Asprey, *War in the Shadows: The Guerilla in History,* 2nd ed., (New York: William Morrow and Company, Inc., 1994) 1098-1099.
[153] Schwarz, 87.
[154] Tommie Sue Montgomery, *Revolution in El Salvador: From Civil Strife to Civil Peace,* 2d ed, (Boulder: Westview Press, 1995), 23.

From mid 1981 to mid 1982, the FMLN consolidated and expanded its position and forces. Additionally, a program of systematic economic destruction and commando attacks against critical military facilities began. Examples of these programs were the destruction of the *Puente de Oro* (Bridge of Gold or Golden Bridge)on the Lempa River and the January 1982 attack on Ilopango air base which damaged or destroyed 15 aircraft, the majority of the El Salvadoran air force.[155]

During this period, the ESAF was committed to static defense and large unit sweep operations. The insurgents maintained the initiative though. President Duarte requested that the US provide a team to do a national military assessment and develop a strategy to defeat the insurgents. A military strategy assistance team, led by Brigadier General Fred Woerner, visited El Salvador in the fall of 1981. The team's report, commonly referred to as the Woerner Report, made a marked impact on the US government and the GOES because it provided a plan to develop the capability of the ESAF. National elections were conducted in 1982, and were protected by the army from the insurgents and corruption. The elections had a significant turnout despite insurgent threats, and subsequently damaged the legitimacy of the FMLN. The elections resulted in a peaceful transition of political power from a military junta to an elected president.

From mid 1982 through 1984, the FMLN launched a series of offensives that dramatically gained the initiative for them. The FMLN began operating in battalion and brigade sized units, from 300 to 1,200 personnel. Their leadership felt the conditions were right to achieve a military victory. The FMLN inflicted severe casualties on the ESAF, and was clearly moving toward military victory. They controlled over 1,000 square miles in northeastern El Salvador, and had attacked over 75 garrisons and villages by the end of 1983.[156]

The ESAF began to expand the size and capability of the army and the air force. Force build up and training allowed it to survive the horrendous casualties it suffered during this period.

---

[155] Byrne, 83 and Bracamonte and Spencer, 140.
[156] Byrne, 85.

From June 1982 to June 1983, the ESAF suffered 2,292 killed, 4,195 wounded and 328 missing, more than twenty percent of the entire force structure.[157]

With significant US pressure and assistance, the National Campaign Plan (NCP) was developed and approved in February 1983. The NCP was to build on the foundation the Woerner Report had provided, and provide the GOES a plan for victory, not just survival. The NCP was designed to fully integrate all elements of national power in order to achieve security in conjunction with development. The plan was to be implemented in two departments, San Vicente and Usulután. However, due to resource constraints, the plan, named Operation*Maquilishuat* (Well Being) by the El Salvadorans, could not be implemented until 10 June 1983 and then only in San Vicente.[158] The NCP was very successful in the first 100 days, but lack of coordination and resources, and failure to successfully implement all aspects denied it ultimate success.

By mid 1984, the rejuvenated ESAF had halted the military advance of the FMLN. The increased military capability and size of the ESAF were beginning to tell against a generally symmetric opponent. The massing of FMLN troops also provided the ability to target them with air power. Additionally, the FMLN hurt itself politically, losing credibility and legitimacy, using forcibly conscripted personnel to replace casualties. Even worse for the insurgents, the elections of 1984 were fair and honest, resulting in another smooth transition of political power to Duarte.

By the end of 1984, the initiative had shifted back to the GOES. The FMLN revisited its strategic assumptions, and finding that the conditions were no longer appropriate to win outright militarily, it began to pursue a strategy of protracted war. Militarily, they maintained the capability to rapidly concentrate, attack a military or economic target of importance, and then disperse before reinforcements arrived. They began to urbanize their force. They continued to attack economic targets. Another aspect of the revised strategy was to try to cause the US to abandon the GOES, in part by intentionally killing US advisors. The attacks on La Unión in

---

[157] Ibid., 108.
[158] Waghelstein, 53.

48

1985, San Miguel cuartel in July 1986, and El Paraíso in March 1987, were intended to kill US advisors. This strategy, along with large amounts of external support from Cuba and Nicaragua, helped the FMLN to regain the overall initiative. They felt the time was right for a new "final" offensive.

The ESAF also recognized the change in the environment, but was not able to shift as easily to a new operational concept as the FMLN. In 1986, the ESAF produced another COIN plan called *Unidos Para Reconstruir* (United to Reconstruct, UPR). The plan encompassed all fourteen departments, where the commanders of the department directed the effort to a local UPR zone. Overall, the UPR, though it was rewritten and approved each year, did not achieve any considerable operational success because of lack of resources and persistence. Additionally, the GOES suffered from a loss of legitimacy due to its inability to effectively enact reforms or govern the country. Presidential elections were held in 1989, and Duarte conducted another smooth transition of civilian authority to the winner, Alfredo Cristiani. Cristiani proposed a plan to open talks with the FMLN in his inaugural address and subsequently began tentative discussions.

However, the talks broke down. On 11 November 1989, the FMLN launched its second "final" offensive, focused primarily in San Salvador, but conducted throughout the country. The offensive achieved strategic surprise against El Salvador and the US since the intelligence assessments concluded the FMLN did not have the strength to conduct such operations. The offensive lasted into December. Never-the-less, the FMLN suffered a military defeat. Once again the offensive did not spark the hoped for popular uprising or defeat the ESAF.

Many consider the 1989 offensive the watershed event that led to the negotiated settlement signed in 1992. First, both sides realized neither could prevail militarily, nor that a prolonged stalemate was a viable long term option. Second, American resolve was shaken and aid called into question after the murder of six Jesuit priests by members of the ESAF during the offensive. Third, the Bush administration, which began in January 1989, indicated to the GOES that it needed to pursue a negotiated settlement. Other external factors also played strongly in the

49

decision to reach a negotiated settlement. The Berlin Wall fell in the winter of 1989, and FMLN

funding from the Soviet Union and its satellite states dried up. In 1990, Violeta Chamorro

became the popularly elected president of Nicaragua, ending 11 years of Sandinista control, and

essentially stopping aid and sanctuary in Nicaragua for the FMLN. The FMLN, weakened by its

1989 offensive, lacking in popular support, and losing external support, fully realized the

importance of a negotiated settlement.

Negotiations proceeded in spurts for the next two years. In October 1990, the US

Congress reduced military aid to El Salvador by 50 percent. In January 1991, the FMLN shot

down a US helicopter and murdered two US servicemen who survived the crash. In response, the

US restored full military aid to El Salvador.[159] In July of 1991, the United Nations Observer

Mission in El Salvador began.[160] Under advice and pressure from the UN Secretary General, the

talks resumed on 16 September in New York and began to make serious progress. After talks in

Mexico City in October and November, the parties returned to New York, where on 1 January

1992, they reached a final agreement. Final issues were ironed out by 12 January and the

Salvadoran Peace Accords were signed on 16 January 1992 in Mexico City.[161]

Analysis of Campaign Planning in El Salvador

The US government had three basic policy goals throughout the conflict in El Salvador:

"(1) combat, deter, and/or defeat the FMLN insurgent threat; (2) strengthen democratic

principles, institutions and structures; and (3) achieve broad-based socioeconomic

development."[162] These goals emerged from 1981 to 1983 and were promulgated in "The Report

of President's National Bipartisan Commission on Central America," more commonly known as

---

[159] Montgomery, 222.
[160] Ibid., 224.
[161] Ibid., 224-225.
[162] Michael Childress, *The Effectiveness of U.S. Training Efforts in Internal Defense and Development: The Cases of El Salvador and Honduras,* (Santa Monica: Rand, 1995), 18.

the Kissinger Report, released in January 1984.[163] Three major campaign plans were developed during the COIN to support all or some of these policy goals: the Woerner Report, in 1981, the National Campaign Plan (NCP) in 1983, and the *Unidos Para Reconstruir* (United to Reconstruct, UPR) plan in 1986.

The Woerner Report (1981)

Following the first FMLN "Final Offensive", US military aid resumed at an increased level and US advisors began to train ESAF infantry battalions. However, to both President Duarte and US Ambassador Deane Hinton, while this assistance provided an effective immediate reaction to the ongoing crisis, there was no overarching concept. In the fall of 1981, the GOES, in coordination with the US Embassy, requested an assessment of the situation to be conducted by US Department of Defense personnel and, in concert with the GOES and ESAF, develop courses of action for defeating the FMLN. As Ambassador Hinton expressed it, he wanted "a basic look at the military situation and what it would take to win."[164] Hinton wanted the head of the assessment team to be at least a Brigadier General (BG) and one who spoke Spanish. From these requests, the El Salvador Military Strategy Assistance Team headed by BG Frederick F. Woerner, Jr. was formed.[165]

The team was composed of seven members: six military members and one civilian intelligence specialist, providing broad coverage of major functional areas. The team had little to no predeployment preparation and only two months to complete the report.[166] Additionally, while the team was composed of members familiar with the US Southern Command area of

[163] Marvin M Gettleman and others, eds, *El Salvador: Central America in the New Cold War,* Revised ed, (New York: Grove Press, 1987), 335.

[164] Max G. Manwaring and Court Prisk, *El Salvador at War: An Oral History from the 1979 Insurrection to the Present,* (Washington, DC: National Defense University Press, 1988), 111-113.

[165] At the time, Woerner was the commander of the 193rd Infantry Brigade.

[166] Ibid., 116. Warner states that he was notified Friday and deployed the following Wednesday, or six days.

responsibility, they were not trained in "strategic planning nor with the development of strategy, " nor was there a doctrinal basis to guide them.[167]

Initially, the team was tasked to develop a comprehensive national COIN plan. However, its charter was reduced to only deal with a national military strategy. Woerner received a letter of instruction that directed him to assist the ESAF *estado mayor* (the Salvadoran high command) in developing this strategy. Woerner perceived as implied tasks the conduct of a military assessment for the US and the development of an outline plan for US security assistance to El Salvador for a period of five years or more.[168] Significantly, Woerner viewed the development of the military strategy prior to the promulgation of a political and economic strategy as skewed in terms of attempting to logically link military objectives to national policy.[169]

Despite his misgivings and with the intent of a national strategy to be developed later, Woerner and his team deployed to El Salvador to produce, within eight weeks, "the most comprehensive study of the Salvadoran military situation ever done."[170] The report had a distinctly Clausewitzian flavor to it as indicated in the opening paragraph of the executive summary which stated, "Military objectives, consistent with the national purpose and interests, were identified and articulated, as were concepts for the attainment of the objectives."[171] Woerner was heavily influenced by Harry Summer's *On Strategy: A Critical Appraisal of the Vietnam War*, and its use of Clausewitz's framework for its analysis, which he had (fortuitously) decided to read on his mission to El Salvador.[172] Of note, Woerner's team did not explicitly define

---

[167] Richard D. Downie, *Learning From Conflict: The U.S. Military in Vietnam, El Salvador, and the Drug War,* (Westport: Praeger, 1998), 133.

[168] Manwaring and Prisk, 115; GEN (RET) Frederick F. Woerner, US Army, former Commander in Chief, US Southern Command, interview by author, 18 February 2003, telephonic, Fort Leavenworth, KS.

[169] GEN (RET) Frederick F. Woerner, US Army, former Commander in Chief, US Southern Command, interview by author, 18 February 2003, telephonic, Fort Leavenworth, KS.

[170] William M. LeoGrande, *Our Own Backyard: The United States in Central America, 1977-1992,* (Chapel Hill: The University of North Carolina Press, 1998), 137.

[171] Frederick F. Woerner, *Report of the El Salvador Military Strategy Assistance Team (Draft),* photocopy of a classified report released with excisions under the Freedom of Information Act, San Salvador, 12 September – 8 November 1981, iii.

[172] Richard D. Downie, "Military Doctrine and the 'Learning Institution:' Case Studies in Low-Intensity Conflict," Ph.D. diss., University of Southern California, 1995, 213, n.35; GEN (RET) Frederick F.

COGs, but focused more critical factors, essentially capabilities to enhance the ESAF as a *system*, and then the use of these enhanced capabilities to degrade the insurgent's systemic capabilities.[173]

Two documents were produced from this process.[174] First, a national military strategy for El Salvador was produced in coordination with the *estado mayor*, which was written in Spanish and remained a classified Salvadoran document. Second, a classified report, which ran several hundred pages, broke the strategy down into two dimensions, preparation for war and conduct of the war. This report was for the US government and never given to the GOES or ESAF.[175] The preparation for war portion dealt with force structure, material and training enhancements required. The warfighting portion dealt with the need to instill offensive, small unit tactics so that "the battle will be taken to the insurgents," and also addressed the protection of elections and economic infrastructure.[176] A concept to implement this strategy was developed. The report warned that the US commitment would be expensive and long term, and provided an outline of the requirements that could not be resourced by the GOES.

The report presented three possible courses of action (COA) for US commitment. The first was a continuation of the strategic defensive, essentially Woerner's throwaway COA, used to demonstrate greater aid was needed since the insurgents could and would maintain their advantage indefinitely. COA Two was an offensive strategy for the ESAF to regain the initiative, but insufficient for victory. COA Three, the most expensive, was titled Strategic Victory, and focused on the destruction of "the insurgents' will and capability to fight."[177] Woerner recommended COA Three, but initially, the Reagan administration was unprepared for the

Woerner, US Army, former Commander in Chief, US Southern Command, interview by author, 18 February 2003, telephonic, Fort Leavenworth, KS..

[173] GEN (RET) Frederick F. Woerner, US Army, former Commander in Chief, US Southern Command, interview by author, 18 February 2003, telephonic, Fort Leavenworth, KS.

[174] GEN (RET) Frederick F. Woerner, US Army, former Commander in Chief, US Southern Command, interview by author, 18 February 2003, telephonic, Fort Leavenworth, KS.

[175] GEN (RET) Frederick F. Woerner, US Army, former Commander in Chief, US Southern Command, interview by author, 18 February 2003, telephonic, Fort Leavenworth, KS.

[176] Woerner, iii.

[177] Ibid., iv.

estimated costs for successful COIN.[178] However, the administration was willing to provide $50 million in military aid the first year. Woerner's team rapidly developed a plan to most effectively use these funds and provided this in the form of a briefing to the Chairman, Joint Chiefs of Staff, for presentation to the President.[179]

The strategy promulgated by the Woerner report was strongly accepted by the ESAF, which viewed it with ownership. The El Salvadorans often credit this strategy for their survival from 1981 to 1985. It provided a blueprint for the US Military Group (MILGP), El Salvador, in the development of their programs and drove increased levels of military aid. More importantly, it forced the recognition on the ESAF that it needed to transform, and provided the impetus and framework to begin that transformation. The strategy was also instrumental in the conduct of fair and honest elections in 1982 and 1984.

The National Campaign Plan (1983)

On 2 February 1983, Colonel John Waghelstein, commander of the MILGP, presented a briefing to high ranking GOES, ESAF, US country team and US Southern Command Officials, which presented options on how to proceed with the war.[180] The options were carefully crafted to guide the Salvadorans from a strictly military prosecution of their civil war to an integrated civil military campaign, where operations could be synchronized in accomplishing overarching objectives. From this meeting derived an El Salvadoran presidential directive that formed a civil-military planning group to design and implement a COIN plan to begin in the departments of San Vicente and Usulután. As an outgrowth of this planning group, the National Commission for

---

[178] Downie, 1998, 133.

[179] GEN (RET) Frederick F. Woerner, US Army, former Commander in Chief, US Southern Command, interview by author, 18 February 2003, telephonic, Fort Leavenworth, KS.

[180] Waghelstein, 52. Attendees included the President of El Salvador, the Minister of Defense of El Salvador, the US Ambassador, and the Deputy Commander in Chief, US Southern Command (Frederick Woerner).

Reconstruction (Comité Nacional de Resturacíon de Areas, CONARA), an inter-ministerial agency, was formed.[181]

The National Campaign Plan (NCP) was a classic IDAD strategy that was based loosely on the Civilian Operations and Revolutionary Development Support (CORDS) program used by the US in Vietnam.[182] It envisioned developmental, humanitarian and civic action programs conducted behind a security screen established by the ESAF and buttressed internally with local civil defense units.[183] The NCP had four priorities (agrarian reform, increased employment, restoration of vital services and humanitarian assistance) and was to be conducted in four phases (planning, offensive, development and consolidation) over a period of three years.[184] The selection of the two provinces was a product of extensive MILGP and country team analysis, instruction, and pressure to get the Salvadorans to prioritize COIN efforts in economically and geographically vital areas of their country, which would affect both the populace and the insurgents. The MILGP focused attention on the "cumulative effects and regional emphasis" of insurgent infrastructure attacks. The Railroad Security Assessment, a report demonstrating the regionalization and effect of insurgent attacks on railroad infrastructure, was an example of this practice.[185] The two provinces were also heavily used as entrance routes for external support to the insurgents.

Operation *Maquilishuat* (Well Being), the initial implementation of the NCP, began 10 June 1983, after delays caused by resource shortages and agency coordination difficulties.[186] The plan was reported to be largely successful in execution for the first 100 days. As Bacevich, et al, (The four colonels) stated, "For its first hundred days, this ambitious project lived up to its promise. The Salvadorans made real headway; they seemed to have broken the code.

---

[181] COL (USA, RET) John Waghelstein, interview by author, 13 February 2003, telephonic, Fort Leavenworth, KS.
[182] LeoGrande, 224.
[183] Manwaring and Prisk, 224.
[184] Waghelstein, 52-53.
[185] Ibid., 51.

Unfortunately, neither the armed forces or the government could sustain the operation."[187] The insurgents launched an offensive in the fall of 1983 that lasted until January 1984. Troops began to be pulled from San Vicente to protect, at least in the American advisors' opinion, areas of secondary importance.[188] The security screen began to become porous and insurgents attacked the program's developmental projects. Though projects continued, sometimes with the permission of the FMLN, for the next two years, essentially, the NCP had failed by early 1994.

The NCP was a significant conceptual leap forward in the conduct of COIN for the ESAF, yet it failed. Many reasons have been given for its failure, most notably: a lack of support by the ESAF since it was perceived as a "gringo plan" or "Made in the USA;" the lack of trained troops; an unwillingness on behalf of the ESAF to train and equip local civil defense forces; a general lack of resources due to shortages and unpredictability of American aid; a lack of Salvadoran interagency and military coordination, Salvadoran and US coordination, and US interagency coordination, and its inability to meet the real needs of the people.[189] However, in accordance with Mintzberg in his *The Rise and Fall of Strategic Planning*, "every failure in implementation is, by definition, a failure in formulation."[190] Clearly, this was the case here. There appeared to be an inability to adapt the plan to address the changing situation, because the original plan did not consider possible branches and sequels. Furthermore, the NCP failed to adequately address resources required versus resources available. However, the planners from the MILGP clearly recognized and identified these weaknesses and struggled to have the ESAF maintain their focus in the NCP area, a task in which they unfortunately failed.[191]

---

[186] Ibid., 53.

[187] Bachevich and others, 44.

[188] Waghelstein, 53.

[189] Byrnes, 109. Downie 1998, 139. Bachevich and others, 44. Montgomery, 168. LeoGrande 224-225.

[190] Henry Mintzberg, *The Rise and Fall of Strategic Planning: Reconceiving Roles for Planning, Plans, Planners*, (New York: The Free Press, 1994), 25.

[191] COL (USA, RET) John Waghelstein, interview by author, 13 February 2003, telephonic, Fort Leavenworth, KS.

Unidos Para Reconstruir (1986)

Unidos Para Reconstruir (UPR) was the offspring of the NCP, but was significantly

different because it was perceived as a Salvadoran plan. It was heavily funded by the US Agency

for International Development (USAID) and consisted of four phases. The UPR attempted to

include all fourteen departments simultaneously with the following stated objectives:

> 1. To win the hearts and minds of the civilian population in order to mobilize its support for the UFR [sic] and unite diverse sectors of the society to develop a solution to the crisis.
> 2. To create an atmosphere of peace and security for the people and protect their well-being in target regions with the goal of beginning a balanced development of the social. Political, and economic sectors of society.
> 3. To destroy the tactical forces of the terrorists in selected regions and neutralize their zones of operations.
> 4. To isolate subversives politically, physically, and psychologically, neutralizing their influence over the civilian population.
> 5. To satisfy the aspirations of the civilian populace in selected areas.
> 6. To incrementally consolidate peace in the country.
> 7. [And] to fortify and consolidate the democratic process at a national level.[192]

The intent was to incorporate all aspects of Salvadoran society in a unified pacification effort,

using the classic *taiche d'huile* methodology. Responsibility fell to military commanders to

establish "UPR zones" in each department, where they could conduct their own COIN programs.

"Fixing the zone's precise location and size was left to the department's military commander in

hopes of enticing him to buy into the scheme."[193] The use of psychological operations was

encouraged for the first time.

The UPR opened its implementation with Operation Phoenix in Guazapa in January 1986

with significant success, but like San Vincente during the NCP, the success could not be

sustained. In October 1986, an earthquake devastated El Salvador, causing tremendous economic

destruction.[194] With the earthquake, the ESAF lost the momentum it had gathered in the initial

---

[192] El Salvadoran Armed Forces, "*Campana de Containsurgencia 'Unidos para Reconstruir'*," (March 1986), 22; quoted in Daniel Siegel and Joy Hackel, "El Salvador: Counterinsurgency Revisited," in *Low Intensity Warfare: Counterinsurgency, Proinsurgency and Antiterrorism in the Eighties*, ed. Michael T. Klare and Peter Kornbluh, 112-135, (New York: Pantheon Books, 1988), 121.
[193] Bacevich and others, 45.
[194] Montgomery, 202. The earthquake registered 7.5 on the Richter scale and caused at least 1,500 deaths.

implementation of the UPR.[195] Regrettably, the UPR, instead of remaining as a national plan, rapidly fragmented into fourteen unrelated and uncoordinated programs competing for sparse resources.[196] Many of the same issues that afflicted the NCP arose again. Even with the expansion of the ESAF to 56,000 by 1987, it lacked the manpower to provide security, conduct offensive operations and perform civic actions. Again, the ESAF failed to develop the local civil defense units it would have needed to provide security and developmental objectives of the UPR listed above.

Even though the UPR was improved every year, it never realized its goal as a national plan. Both the Salvadorans and Americans realized that the Salvadorans needed to promulgate national political objectives from which to base a national plan, but were never able to do so. In large part, the Americans blamed this on an organizational deficiency in the GOES, postulating they needed a National Security Council equivalent.[197] The Salvadorans criticized the Americans for not providing the training and advice required to achieve synchronization of the UPR.[198]

Conclusions

> Mr. President, I offer a toast to the Salvadoran people: may they soon come to enjoy the
> long deferred peace and prosperity they deserve.
> -Vice President George H.W. Bush[199]

For the GOES and the US, the negotiated settlement that ended the war in El Salvador must be viewed as a policy victory. El Salvador did not fall to a Marxist insurgency, democracy was progressing and socio-economic development was also advancing. With the peace treaty in place, greater resources could be applied against economic and social development. While the three COIN campaign plans had a tremendous positive and cumulative impact on the civil war in El Salvador, they were not planned or executed appropriately to directly win the victory for the GOES. For an example of this positive and cumulative impact, politically motivated deaths by

---

[195] Manwaring and Prisk, 346-348.
[196] Bacevich and others, 45; Downie 1998, 141.
[197] Manwaring and Prisk, 472-473
[198] Victor Rosello, "Lessons From El Salvador," *Parameters* 23, no. 4 (Winter 1993-94), 107.

security forces fell from an estimated 10,000 in 1980 to 100 in 1990. This decline is more dramatically shown in monthly rates from an average of 750 in 1980, to 22 in 1986, to eight in 1990.[200] Over a ten year period, this shows an exponential decrease, and essentially illustrates a change from the institutionally accepted conduct of political violence to individually executed political violence.

In regards to the campaign plans themselves, the military strategy developed by Woerner and his team allowed El Salvador first to survive as a state, and then provide the capability that allowed the state to no longer be threatened by an insurgent military takeover. The NCP provided a huge conceptual leap forward in terms of integrated, prioritized and focused civil military operations. As stated by Bacevich, et al, "The Woerner report had aimed to create an army that could kill guerillas; *the aim of the NCP was to win* [emphasis added]."[201] Unfortunately, the NCP was over ambitious in its understanding of the ESAF's operational reach. The UPR attempted to maintain the goals of the NCP, but with a Salvadoran flavor. However, it never fulfilled its role as a unified national plan. Victor Rosello identifies this lack of a unifying and unified national plan as the significant factor in denying the GOES its victory. He states,

> Had the Salvadoran Joint Command prepared a strategic plan that integrated strategic, operational, and tactical objectives, coordinated into multiple inter-zonal operations, the military might have defeated the FMLN on the battlefield. Part of the blame for this shortcoming must be shared by the US military advisory mission for not providing more professional advice at the operational and strategic levels. For whatever reasons, training and advice remained predominantly tactical. The military advisory mission might have influenced ESAF attitudes in this respect through more aggressive support at the level of national and military strategy.[202]

---

[199] Bush Toast, San Salvador, 1983.
[200] Childress, 36.
[201] Bacevich and others, 21.
[202] Rosello, 107.

COMPARATIVE ANALYSIS OF THE COUNTERINSURGENCY CAMPAIGNS

All guerilla movements have many characteristics in common – just as each has its virtually unique features. The similarities and dissimilarities owe far more to human similarities and differences than to the physical environment. *It is difficult to determine which is the more dangerous and expensive error for the counterguerilla operator – failure to recognize the characteristics common to most or all guerilla movements, or failure to recognize those that are virtually unique to the movement it is his duty to oppose* [emphasis added].

-COL Napoleon Valeriano and LTC Charles Bohannan[203]

Countering the Huk insurgency in the Philippines is often considered "the" unique case study due to the emergence of Ramon Magsaysay. However, this is too simplistic a view, and powerful lessons can be drawn from the Philippines, particularly when it is used as an "experimental control" for planning a successful COIN campaign. A comparative analysis of the COIN campaigns presented previously illustrates the similarities and uniqueness of each situation, and the implications that elicits for both campaign planning for COIN and the conduct of COIN itself.

Similarities

In comparing the two counterinsurgencies, four areas of similarity are particularly significant for campaign planning: the criticality of US advisory assistance and aid; the use of this aid as leverage to promote US strategic goals; the effect of honest, free elections; and the protracted nature of the conflicts.

Criticality of US Advisory Assistance and Aid

US advisory assistance and aid was critical in the conduct of both counterinsurgencies, but was not decisive in the defeat of the insurgency in either. US assistance was decisive in preventing the military defeat of the contested governments by the insurgent forces. In both El Salvador and the Philippines, US aid and training which allowed the expansion of the military

---

[203] Valeriano and Bohannan, 15.

force sizes and capabilities allowed the governments to survive. However, in the Philippines, the advice and aid provided critical support to a strategic concept already developed by Magsaysay. In El Salvador, it is questionable whether an overarching strategic concept ever existed, which led in part to the necessity of a negotiated solution.

Significantly, provision of US advisory assistance and aid does not require a major presence in the country. In both countries, the US military footprint was extremely small, roughly fifty five in El Salvador and at its peak, fifty seven in the Philippines.[204] Additionally, military trainers were generally not allowed to accompany host nation units on combat missions.[205] While the relatively small size and prohibition of combat created some problems in US assistance, they were not insurmountable in the overall conduct of the COIN effort.[206]

Use of Aid as Leverage to Promote US Strategic Goals

The US government directly and indirectly used economic and military aid to promote the achievement of its strategic goals in both situations. The amount of leverage the US government successfully directly applied was tied to the decisive impact of that aid. The signed, personal agreement between Presidents Truman and Quirino over the fiscal responsibility of the Philippines government highlights this factor. In El Salvador, (then) Vice-President George H.W. Bush's toast during a state visit in 1983, where continued aid was overtly threatened if human rights progress was not made, was another indicator. Indirect leverage was exercised through advisors like Lansdale, Waghelstein and Woerner, who, through trust, teaching, mentoring and

---

[204] While the 55 man presence in El Salvador is slightly misleading due to the means of how military personnel were counted, US military presence never exceeded approximately 150 personnel even at the height of involvement, still an extremely small footprint. For the Philippines, 57 was the size of the JUSMAG since there existed forward based US forces not involved in the counterinsurgency effort.
[205] In the Philippines, Lansdale and Bohannan were the only advisors allowed to accompany AFP combat missions until 1953. In 1953, the JCS made the decision to allow US advisors to accompany their units as observers and not combatants. In El Salvador, US advisors were never allowed to accompany ESAF units in combat, but the Defense Attaches assigned to the US Embassy could.
[206] COL (USA, RET) John Waghelstein, interview by author, 13 February 2003, telephonic, Fort Leavenworth, KS. COL Waghelstein felt that the predominantly tactical focus of the advisors was driven by the 55 man limit. While he feels that, "small is beautiful," he felt that advisors assigned down to the battalion level would have been appropriate, allowing brigade advisors to focus on higher level training and planning.

advising, were able to focus aid to programs that furthered US policy while achieving acceptance and buy-in by the host nations.

In terms of COIN campaign planning, it is important to recognize that assistance and aid provide access into the host nation and their planning efforts. However, except under the most dire of circumstances, it does not provide the US with sufficient direct leverage to force significant reform or even acceptance of strategic or operational direction of a campaign plan. This is best obtained through indirect leverage, which requires the substantial commitment and perseverance of US advisors in the creation of professional relationships of trust and respect. Substantial improvements in terms of military capability, subordination of the military to civilian control, and the respect of human rights were achieved in the Philippines and El Salvador through the indirect leverage provided by US advisors.

The Effect of Honest, Free Elections

The impact of multiple, nonfradulent national elections was significant in both the Philippines and El Salvador. As the exponent of the Cuban revolutionary model, Che Guevara stated, "Where a government has come into power through some form of popular vote, fraudulent or not, and maintains at least an appearance of constitutional legality, the guerilla outbreak cannot be promoted, since the possibilities of peaceful struggle have not yet been exhausted."[207] The honest elections created a perception of the legitimacy of the existent governments and the possibility of nonviolent, political solution to the underlying causes of the insurgencies.

Significantly, in both cases, major planning efforts were conducted to ensure nonfradulent elections, and subsequently to publicize the honesty with which the elections were conducted, to gain an advantage over the insurgents through informational means. Additionally, in both cases, greater effect was achieved by multiple, subsequent honest elections, which indicated both domestically and internationally that a measure of reform had taken root. The

---

[207] Ernesto "Che" Guevara, *Guerilla Warfare*, (New York: Monthly Review Press, 1961; reprint, Lincoln: University of Nebraska Press, 1985), 48 (page citations are to reprint edition).

legitimacy provided to the governments of the Philippines and El Salvador by multiple honest elections facilitated the surrender and reintegration of Huk insurgents and the negotiated settlement in El Salvador, respectively.

Protracted Nature of the Conflicts

Both insurgencies lasted an extended period of time. In El Salvador, the insurgency is generally considered to have lasted 11 years, from 1981 to 1992. The insurgency in the Philippines has a much less definitive end date and start date, but the Huk rebellion is generally considered to have lasted thirteen or so years, from 1946 to 1960.

In terms of planning, the length of the insurgency makes a tremendous impact. In both cases, the insurgents transitioned their forms of warfare at least once (from mobile warfare to guerilla warfare), requiring a different approach by the counterinsurgent forces also. Additionally, the protracted nature of COIN has serious policy level impacts on the counterinsurgent forces in terms of force structure, terms of service, and training.

Dissimilarities

The dissimilarities exhibited by the two case studies also illustrate significant lessons for the COIN campaign planner. The major dissimilarities are the emergence of a leader as the essential link of the COIN, the reintegration of insurgents into society and the respect of human rights, the political power of the armed forces, the impact external support of the insurgency, and impact of immediate strategic guidance.

Emergence of a Leader

The emergence of Ramon Magsaysay as the focal point of COIN in the Philippines was a unique occurrence. To find leaders like him in other COIN situations became the chimerical pursuit of US COIN practice that continues to the current day. Too often, the US confused the local strong man with a selfless, effective and honest leader like Magsaysay. The same can be said of those expressing the desire to rule legitimately, but lacking the power to do so effectively.

63

This was manifested with President Duarte in El Salvador, who lacked the power to end corruption within the government, execute land reform, or effectively prosecute human rights violators from the ESAF.

While the emergence of a Magsaysay needs to be recognized as singleton point of datum, the pursuit of effective leadership and unity of effort cannot be ignored and should be facilitated through COIN campaign planning. Free elections, as discussed above, are a primary means to pursue effective leadership. In El Salvador, while US hopes clearly rested with the success of Duarte, the continued conduct of honest, free elections enhanced the perception of governmental legitimacy, and lead to the eventual settlement of the insurgency through political agreement following the election of Alfredo Cristaini.

Reintegration of Insurgents into Society and the Respect of Human Rights

A key recognition by the Magsaysay was that the Huks were part of Philippine society and consequently, for a lasting peace to exist, needed to be reintegrated back into society or eliminated completely. Thus, from the beginning, the plan in the Philippines called for "All Out Friendship or All Out Force." COIN activities focused on forcing a separation between the Filipino society and the insurgents, as such, forcing them to choose reintegration into society or destruction. Programs like EDCORPS, and the accompanying informational efforts, demonstrated that the government was willing to fairly pardon insurgents, as well as address the social issues which had fueled the insurgency. The Philippine campaign also focused on applying the rule of law to all people, largely through the respect of human rights. Many of the reforms Magsaysay instituted immediately dealt with issues such as raising the pay of soldiers, bringing the constabulary under military control, and suspending the writ of *habeas corpus*. However, for these efforts to be successful, the AFP also needed to prove itself effective against the Huks in the "all out force" arena, which it had achieved by the end of 1951.

On the other hand in El Salvador, the GOES and ESAF perceived the FMLN as an enemy to be destroyed. The need to reintegrate the insurgents did not occur until the election of Cristiani in 1988, which subsequently led to the negotiated conclusion of the insurgency. Even when the peace treaty was signed there was deep concern that the ESAF would not accept it. This was also reflected in their perceived lack of respect for human rights. At the beginning of the insurgency, political executions were an institutionally acceptable way to deal with dissent. While the scope of these deaths dropped exponentially over the course of the war and institutional change seemed to have occurred, there were still substantial political deaths perpetrated by the security forces until the peace treaty was signed.

Political Power of the Armed Forces

The ESAF was one of the primary sources of political power in El Salvador. It had essentially controlled the executive branch of the government since the 1930s, and strongly impacted economic and judiciary policy. Thus, in many ways, until at least 1984, the president of El Salvador served at the pleasure of the military instead of vice versa. This strongly impacted the COIN campaign. This impact is illustrated by the failure of the UPR through resources being spread equitably through the areas of the Brigade commanders versus being focused were they might have had the most impact. This also was illustrated through attempted judiciary prosecutions for human rights abusers, which were consistently foiled by the ESAF. However, one of the most significant reforms of the ESAF was the acceptance of subordination to the office of the country's executive instead of the man who held the office.

In the Philippines, the AFP did not wield the political power the ESAF did. Subsequently, Magsaysay was able to force his will upon the military and create rapid reforms. The power he exercised as minister of defense to relieve senior officers and replace them with vigorous junior officers was a power no civilian in El Salvador possessed. Additionally, his ability to impose his policies, like the Army Attraction Program, greatly facilitated the institutional respect for human rights and the perception of governmental legitimacy.

External Support of the Insurgency

External support to the insurgency was not a significant issue in the conduct of the Philippines insurgency, and was subsequently rarely addressed by the Filipino and US counterinsurgents.[208] However, external support was significant and a major factor in the protracted insurgency in El Salvador. Bracamonte and Spencer estimate that the FMLN received close to $1 billion in external support from 1980 to 1992.[209] Cuba and Nicaragua provided the majority of the support, and not just weapons and funds, but sanctuary and training facilities as well. Additionally, Cuba and Nicaragua acted as clearinghouses to funnel other external support to the FMLN. These other sources of support included nation states like Vietnam, the Soviet Union, Algeria, Ethiopia, and Yugoslavia, and transnational actors like the PLO, the Basque ETA, and other terrorist organizations.[210]

Significantly for planners, the US and the GOES never addressed external support of the insurgency as part of their COIN campaign plans. Interdiction was viewed almost exclusively as a military action, with the Salvadoran Navy having the lead role.[211] Exercise of the other elements of national power against the sources of external support was neither actively pursued nor effectively coordinated in any way, and certainly not integrated in any COIN campaign plan. The existence of these channels of external support and sanctuary allowed the FMLN to persist even as their popular support within El Salvador declined. Clearly, significant diplomatic and

---

[208] The Huks received minor financial aid from communist parties worldwide. The majority of any money received came from (or at least through) the US. Additionally, the Huks received some minor assistance from the Chinese communists primarily in training and organization.

[209] Bracamonte and Spencer, 6-7.

[210] Ibid.

[211] COL (USA, RET) John Waghelstein, interview by author, 13 February 2003, telephonic, Fort Leavenworth, KS. Significant progress was made by the Salvadoran Navy, but a joint effort was nearly impossible to create. Additionally, while San Vicente and Usulután were major transshipment areas for external support, this was a negligible factor in their selection for the initial conduct of the NCP.

informational efforts should have been planned, integrated and executed as part of the overall COIN effort.

Immediate Strategic Guidance

Once the US realized the magnitude of the insurgency in the Philippines, policy and strategic guidance was rapidly and clearly articulated through NSC 84/2 in November 1950. The importance of the Philippines was defined in terms of US national security, and ends, ways, means, and risks were presented. US aid to the Philippines was facilitated. Leverage was exerted for economic aid by requiring demonstrations of increased governmental efficiency and legitimacy. While human rights were not explicitly addressed, societal reform was identified as an objective. This clear strategic guidance allowed the US advisors and senior US officials in country to assist in counterinsurgent planning and programming resources for local actions, which facilitated the achievement of operational and strategic objectives.

On the other hand, in El Salvador US strategic policy was slower in articulation and less clear in content. US policy emerged over a period of three years, through documents like the Woerner Report and the NCP, and finally articulated fully with the release of the Kissinger Report in early 1984. The lack of definitive guidance presented problems for operational planning.

Conclusion

The similarities and differences highlighted above clearly illustrate possible universals in the conduct of COIN operations, as well as the uniqueness of each situation. As a planner, no static checklist of planning considerations will apply to every case. As Colonels Valeriano and Bohannan stated at the beginning of this section, it is essential not to fail to identify the commonalities as well as the differences. Thus, critical to planners is a detailed understanding of the operational environment in order to clearly recognize possible similarities and dissimilarities from historical cases that could assist in creating a counterinsurgent campaign plan.

67

CONCLUSIONS AND RECOMMENDATIONS

General Conclusions

In its broadest outline, the three stage process of joint operational design is generally sufficient to address COIN campaign planning. From the examination of the case studies, the methodology used during both counterinsurgencies mirrored the joint process, which generally followed a path of perception (or formulation) of strategic guidance, identification of critical factors, and the subsequent development of an operational concept, guided by the critical factors to achieve the strategic objectives. Where the joint model does not support counterinsurgent campaign planning is within the details of the three stages themselves, and will be addressed below in the specific conclusions.

Additionally, there are operational shortfalls in the planning for COIN. US COIN doctrine was largely developed during the 1960s and has passed to the present virtually unchanged. Joint appreciation of operational art emerged in the armed forces of the US during the 1980s. However, the operational level of war is still primarily viewed through the lens of mid and high intensity conflict. COIN in theory and doctrine has yet to be reexamined in terms of operational art and needs to be.

Specific Conclusions

Integrated Campaign Plan at the Operational Level

The planning and conduct of the COIN campaign requires full integration of the elements of national power at the operational level, instead of the strategic level. For the US, this translates to joint and interagency integration and coordination in planning and execution of the COIN campaign plan to achieve significant increases in effectiveness. Achieving unity effort through operational integration allows the production of synergistic effects caused by synchronized actions throughout the depths of the battlespace.

In the Philippines by 1951, there was generally good integration of the elements of national power, largely brought about by the leadership of Magsaysay, serving as Secretary of Defense and subsequently as President. Military, political and economic actions were integrated to maximize military, social and political effects and enhancing the Philippine government's legitimacy. Magsaysay recognized that defeating the insurgents required the government assert its moral right to govern. This required successful military suppression of the insurgents, and addressing the fundamental causes of the insurgency. Addressing the root causes of the insurgency required government resources outside the realm of the military, as well as the creative adaptation of the military to provide the assistance. Further, this was conducted under the rubric of a comprehensive and synergistic information effort such that all positive government action was advertised to achieve greater effect.

Operational Art for Counterinsurgency

As stated earlier, the language of operational art was not primarily designed for low intensity conflict. The facets of operational art, as defined by joint doctrine, apply conceptually to COIN, but need to be refined through examination of the COIN environment. As shown in the Philippine campaign, synergy plays a crucial role in linking tactical actions, civic actions and informational efforts. Tempo also plays a different role in the COIN environment based on the probable protracted nature of the conflict. Center of gravity may require some reinterpretation. In both case studies, center of gravity was viewed primarily as a strategic element in traditional terms, and expressed in COIN truisms like "the people" or "popular support." At the operational level, the government and its security forces and the insurgent forces are viewed essentially as systems, without articulating a center of gravity. Operational objectives took the form of the enhancement and degradation of capabilities, isolation and separation from the population and domination of human terrain. The concept of simultaneity may also require reexamination in terms of an integrated campaign plan. Actions integrating the elements of national power should occur concurrently, indicating a greater harmony of purpose, and affecting the insurgents along military and nonmilitary fronts. Additionally, lines of operations need to be examined in physical and logical lines to help achieve concurrence of integrated actions.

Long Term Commitment

Critical to any COIN campaign plan is the consideration of the need of a long term commitment. This impacts in a number of ways. First, it has informational and diplomatic impacts. Diplomatically, the dedication exhibited in long term commitments enhances the status of the US to its allies. It also requires the conduct of an informational effort to maintain positive public, international and domestic political opinion in order to sustain the commitment. This in turn impacts on how resources are programmed and the manner and order that objectives and subobjectives are pursued and obtained at the operational and national levels. Execution of a long term commitment allows the possibility of significant cultural changes to be planned for and executed, such as in ending institutionally accepted human rights abuse in El Salvador. Finally, it requires that COIN campaign planning be event driven, with clearly articulated measures of progress and success.

Aid for Access and Leverage

US aid is an essential element in US COIN advisory because it provides access into the host nation's planning process. In both case studies, US advisory assistance and aid played a crucial role in the ultimate success of the counterinsurgent forces. US aid allowed indirect pressure to be applied to the host nation to reform or to provide guidance in a noncoercive, persuasive manner. The use of aid to gain direct leverage has been largely ineffective, however. Generally, if the US is willing to provide aid, then its security interests are at risk. Therefore, it would be harmful to those interests to reduce or stop aid. The challenge for the operational planner is that direct leverage is usually only effective when US security interests are relatively minor.

Recommendations

Further Study of Counterinsurgency in Terms of Operational Art

With the ongoing War on Terrorism as impetus, the theory and doctrine of COIN require reexamination in terms of operational art. The needs for planning and executing COIN must be examined in detail and included in operational level doctrinal manuals, especially the joint publications that deals with campaign planning. Additionally, COIN must be examined to address new and emergent forms of insurgency. Other operational concepts for COIN are needed if the internal defense and development model is no longer sufficient. The creation of either a joint publication or a joint tactics, techniques and procedures manual for COIN campaign planning is needed.

In recognizing the importance of the operational study of COIN, efforts should be made to include COIN as a topic of study or increase the time currently dedicated to its instruction in the Services' war colleges, operational planning schools, and the command and staff colleges. The probable future conduct of COIN campaigns further requires the services to recognize that COIN is a joint requirement and not merely a requirement of the special operation forces.

Situational Understanding of the Operational Environment

Consideration should be given to adding a fourth stage in the operational design model to provide the planner situational understanding of the operational environment. Currently, this is partially incorporated in joint intelligence preparation of the battlefield, which occurs primarily during the identification of critical factors. However, the complex nature of the operational environment in COIN and the need to achieve unity of effort of the elements among national power through an integrated campaign plan indicate the greater need for understanding this operational environment. This importance would indicate the need to separately articulate the research and understanding of the operational environment as its own stage in the operational design model.

Defining Progress in Counterinsurgency

How progress in defined in the conduct of COIN must initially be clearly defined by the campaign planners during the development of their product. This requires a clear understanding of the operational environment as well as the strategic guidance. However, these measures of success must not be viewed merely as static indicators, but require refinement and redirection as the situation evolves. In both case studies presented, the insurgents shifted from mobile to guerilla warfare, which caused counterinsurgent measures of effectiveness to change. The ability to rapidly identify and adapt these measures facilitated the ultimate success of the governments.

The other major considerations in defining progress are the necessity of time to create lasting cultural change and examining progress in relative versus absolute terms. In many ways these considerations are linked, as illustrated by the decrease in human rights violations in El Salvador discussed previously. US presence and training, in conjunction with leverage based upon aid, was largely responsible for this decrease. The institutional change took a significant amount of time to produce, and in absolute terms could be deemed inadequate. However, in relative terms, the effort must be considered extremely successful.

Victory in Counterinsurgency

The concept of victory in COIN needs to be examined in light of it being principally a nonmilitary conflict. The American way of war is based upon unconditional surrender, but the military defeat of insurgent forces is only a partial solution, and may not lead tolong term amelioration of the root causes. As such, victory needs to be defined in terms of stability, the ability to establish a lasting peaceful conclusion, and the strategic benefits these provide to the US and the HN. This concept was clearly captured in NSC 84/2, which states as an objective for the Philippines, "An effective government which will preserve and strengthen the pro-U.S. orientation of the people."[212] This largely encompassed stability, lasting solution and US

---

[212] U.S. National Security Council Staff, "A Report to the President by the National Security Council with Respect to the Philippines," NSC 84/2, 9 November 1950, in *The Philippines Reader: A History of*

strategic advantage. Further, it is the responsibility of the planner to recognize the concept of

victory in COIN, and also to be able to educate senior commanders and policy makers. At a

practical level, the definition of victory will be specific to each COIN situation, and will define

the importance of US interests as well as the limits of US power in achieving these interests.

Effects-Based Operations for Counterinsurgency

EBO is an emerging operational design concept. As defined by COL (USAF, Ret) Mann

et al, "EBO represents those actions taken against enemy systems designed to achieve specific

that contribute directly to desired military and political outcomes."[213] EBO is based on systems

thinking and forces the planner to consider the downstream impact of his actions. Further, EBO

is designed to be an inherently integrated methodology to apply all the elements of national

power. Unfortunately, like operational art itself, EBO has been explored primarily in terms of

interstate armed conflict, a deficiency identified in many of the current works. EBO is also the

basis of Rapid Decisive Operations, a veritable anathema to the COIN campaign planner.

However, EBO offers great potential for future use as a construct for COIN campaign

planning. First, it is designed to plan for and exercise all the elements of national power. This

should facilitate the close integration that COIN requires, particularly between the military and

the informational elements. Second, it forces planners to fully consider second and third order

effects, and subsequently reduce the unintended consequences which can be particularly

devastating in the conduct of COIN. Third, as shown in the two case studies, much of the

operational planning was done by essentially viewing the opposing forces as systems and then

creating effects which enhanced your own system or degraded the enemy's.

EBO still requires further refinement for successful application in COIN campaign

planning. One of the largest deficiencies is the lack of examination of the creation of positive or

---

Colonialism, Neocolonialism, Dictatorship and Resistance, ed. Daniel B. Schirmer and Stephen R. Shalom, (Boston: South End Press, 1987), 110.

73

enhancing effects. Nearly all the work done in EBO deals with degradation of the enemy's system. However, in COIN, the enhancement of your own system is usually critical, as is influencing and dominating uncommitted human terrain through enhancing the legitimacy of your system in the perception of the populace. Another significant deficiency in EBO lies in the lack of methodology to laterally link concurrent or simultaneous effects to produce greater synergism in achieving operational or strategic objectives. Additionally, EBO requires a detailed understanding of the operational environment to effectively employ this methodology. Finally, an EBO-based COIN campaign plan would require a near continuous stream of fine grained intelligence to track measures of progress and determine success.

The Future of Counterinsurgency Campaign Planning

This monograph has illustrated there is a significant body of knowledge on campaign design that can be applied to counterinsurgency. The joint campaign planning model provides an appropriate outline. There is an immediate need to reexamine US COIN doctrine in terms of operational art to address shortfalls. It is critical counterinsurgent forces develop integrated, coherent campaign plans, recognizing the need to win the information war for legitimacy, that address the underlying cause of the insurgencies. The challenge remains to define an integrated operational concept which fully articulates persuasive and coercive elements, through the application of all the elements of national power, into campaign design.

---

[213] Edward C. Mann, III, Gary Endersby, and Thomas R. Searle, *Thinking Effects: Effects-Based Methodology for Joint Operations*, CADRE Paper No. 15, (Maxwell Air Force Base: Air University Press, 2002), 1.

Appendix A: The Facets of Operational Art

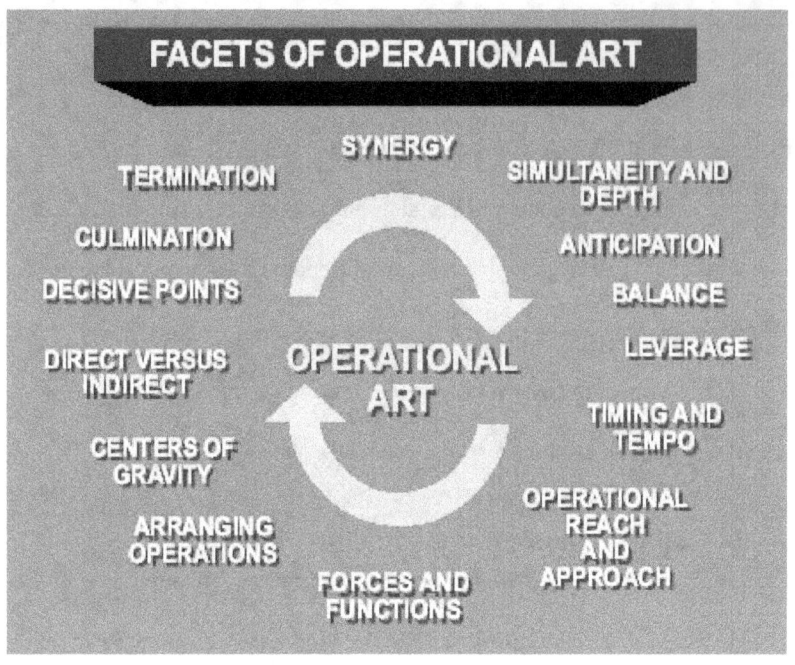

Figure 1: The Facets of Operational Art[214]

---
[214] Joint Publication 3-0, III-10.

Appendix B: Internal Defense and Development Strategy Model

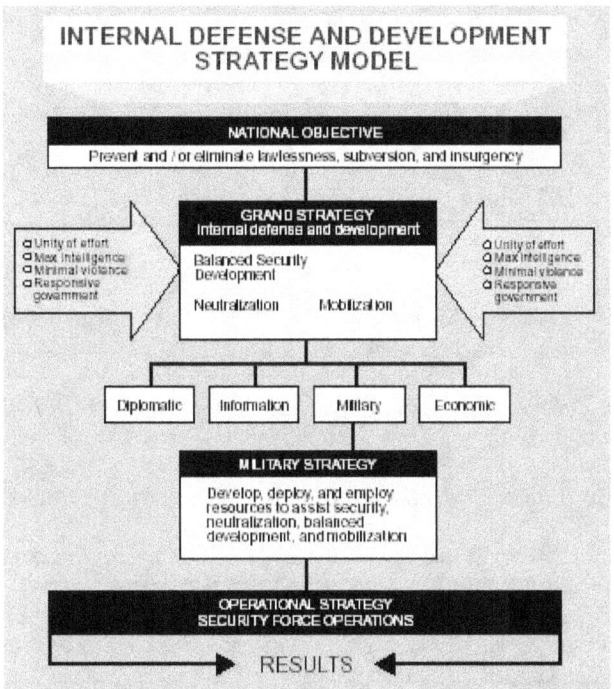

Figure 2: Internal Defense and Development Strategy Model[215]

---

[215] Joint Publication 3-07.1, C-2.

BIBLIOGRAPHY

Asprey, Robert B. *War in the Shadows: The Guerilla in History.* 2 vols. Garden City: Doubleday and Company, Inc., 1975.

_____. *War in the Shadows: The Guerilla in History.* 2nd ed. New York: William Morrow and Company, Inc., 1994.

Bacevich, A.J., James D. Hallums, Richard H. White, and Thomas F. Young. *American Policy in Small Wars: The Case of El Salvador* (Special Report). Washington, D.C.:Pergamon-Brassey's, 1988.

Barrens, Clarence G. "I Promise: Magsaysay's Unique PSYOP 'Defeats' Huks." Masters Thesis. U.S. Army Command and General Staff College, 1970.

Becker, Michael, D. *Operational Art in Counterinsurgency Campaign Planning.* Newport: Department of Operations, Naval War College, 17 June 1994. DTIC, ADA 283523.

Beckett, Ian F.W. *Encyclopedia of Guerilla Warfare.* New York: Checkmark Books, 2001.

_____. "Forward to the Past: Insurgency in Our Midst," *Harvard International Review* 23, no. 2 (Summer 2001): 59-63.

_____. *Modern Insurgencies and Counter-insurgencies: Guerillas and their Opponents since 1750.* London: Routledge, 2001.

_____, ed. *The Roots of Counter-Insurgency: Armies and Guerilla Warfare, 1900-1945.* London: Blanford Press, 1988.

Birtle, Andrew, J. *U.S. Army Counterinsurgency and Contingency Operations Doctrine 1860-1941.* Washington, DC: Center of Military History, 1998.

Blaufarb, Douglas S. *The Counterinsurgency Era: U.S. Doctrine and Performance.* NewYork: The Free Press, 1977.

Bracamonte, José A.M. and David E. Spencer. *Strategy and Tactics of the Salvadoran FMLN Guerillas: Last Battle of the Cold War, Blueprint for Future Conflicts.* Wesport: Praeger, 1995.

Brockerhoff, Martin P. "An Urbanizing World," *Population Bulletin* 55, No. 3, (September 2000), 48 pages. Site at http://www.prb.org/Template.cfm?Section= PRB&template=/ContentManagement/ContentDisplay.cfm&ContentID=5886. Accessed on 12 December 2002.

Byrne, Hugh. *El Salvador's Civil War: A Study of Revolution.* Boulder: Lynne Rienner Publishers, 1996.

Bunge, Frederica M. *Philippines: A Country Study.* Washington, DC: U.S. Government Printings Office, DA PAM 550-72, 1984.

Cable, Larry E. *Conflict of Myths: The Development of American Counterinsurgency Doctrine and the Vietnam War.* New York: New York University Press, 1986.

_____. "Reinventing the Round Wheel: Insurgency, Counter-Insurgency, and Peacekeeping Post Cold War," *Small Wars and Insurgencies* 4, no. 2 (Autumn 1993): 228-262.

Callwell, Charles E. *Small Wars: Their Principles and Practice,* 3d ed. London: His Majesty's Stationary Office, 19XX. Reprint, Lincoln: University of Nebraska Press, 1996.

Campbell, Arthur. *Guerillas: A History and Analysis.* New York: The John Day Company, 1968.

Central Intelligence Agency. "El Salvador" in *The World Factbook 2002.* 1 January 2002. Site at http://www.cia.gov/cia/publications/factbook/geos/es.html. Accessed on 30 January 2003.

Central Intelligence Agency. "Philippines" in *The World Factbook 2002.* 1 January 2002. Site at http://www.cia.gov/cia/publications/factbook/geos/es.html. Accessed on 17 February 2003.

Chapman, William. *Inside the Philippine Revolution.* New York: W.W. Norton & Company, 1987.

Childress, Michael. *The Effectiveness of U.S. Training Efforts in Internal Defense and Development: The Cases of El Salvador and Honduras.* Santa Monica: Rand, 1995.

Clausewitz, Carl von. *On War.* Edited and translated by Michael Howard and Peter Paret. Princeton: Princeton University Press, 1976.

Comish, Leo S., Jr. "The United States and the Philippine Hukbalahap Insurgency: 1946-1954." USAWC Research Paper, US Army War College, 1971.

de Wijk, Rob. "The Limits of Military Power," *The Washington Quarterly* 25: 1 (Winter 2002): 75-92.

Dillon, Dana R. "Comparative Counter-insurgency Strategies in the Phillipines," *Small Wars and Insurgencies* 6, no. 3 (Winter 1995): 281-303.

Downie, Richard D. *Learning From Conflict: The U.S. Military in Vietnam, El Salvador, and the Drug War.* Westport: Praeger, 1998.

_____. "Military Doctrine and the 'Learning Institution:' Case Studies in Low-Intensity Conflict." Ph.D. diss., University of Southern California, 1995.

Eisenhower, Dwight D. *Crusade in Europe.* Garden City: Doubleday and Company, Inc., 1948. Reprint, Pennington: Collectors Reprints, Inc., 1996.

El Salvadoran Armed Forces. *"Campana de Containsurgencia 'Unidos para Reconstruir'."* March 1986, 22. Quoted in Daniel Siegel and Joy Hackel, "El Salvador: Counterinsurgency Revisited," in *Low Intensity Warfare: Counterinsurgency,*

Proinsurgency and Antiterrorism in the Eighties, ed. Michael T. Klare and Peter Kornbluh, 112-135. New York: Pantheon Books, 1988, 121.

Fall, Bernard B. *Last Reflections on a War.* Garden City, New York: Doubleday & Company, Inc., 1975.

Field Manual 5-0 (Final Draft). *Army Planning and Orders Production.* 15July 2002.

Gettleman, Marvin M., Patrick Lacefield, Louis Menashe and David Mermelstin, eds. *El Salvador: Central America in the New Cold War,* Revised ed. New York: Grove Press, 1987.

Golay, Frank, H. *The Philippines: Public Policy and National Economic Development.* Ithaca: Cornell University Press, 1961, 71-72. Quoted in Dana R. Dillon, "Comparative Counter-insurgency Strategies in the Phillipines," *Small Wars and Insurgencies* 6, no. 3, 285, (Winter 1995).

Grant, Thomas A. "Government, Politics, and Low-Intensity Conflict." In *Low-Intensity Conflict: Old Threats in a New World.* ed. Edwin G. Corr and Stephan Sloan, 257-275. Westview Studies in Regional Security, ed. Wm. J. Olson. Boulder: Westview Press, 1992.

_____. "Little Wars, Big Problems: The United States and Counterinsurgency in the Postwar World." Ph.D. diss., University of California, Irving, 1990.

Greenberg, Lawrence M. *The Hukbalahap Insurrection: A Case Study of a Successful Anti-Insurgency Operation in the Philippines, 1946-1955.* Washington, DC: Analysis Branch US Army Center of Military History, CMH Pub 93-8, 1986.

Greer, James K. "Operational Art for the Objective Force," *Military Review* 82, no. 5 (October 2002): 22-29.

Guevara, Ernesto "Che". *Guerilla Warfare.* New York: Monthly Review Press, 1961. Reprint, Lincoln: University of Nebraska Press, 1985.

Gurr, Ted Robert. *Why Men Rebel.* Princeton: Princeton University Press, 1970.

Hammer, Kenneth. "Huks in the Philippines," *Military Review* 36, no. 1, (April 1956): 50-54.

Holland, John. *Hidden Order: How Adaptation Builds Complexity.* Reading: Helix Books, 1995.

Institute for International Mediation and Conflict Resolution. "The World Conflict and Human Rights Map 2001." Site at http://www.iimcr.org/imgs/Conflictmap %202001-g.pdf. Accessed on 31 December 2002.

International Monetary Fund Staff. "Globalization: Threat or Opportunity?" April 12, 2000 (Corrected January 2002). Site at http://www.imf.org/external/np/exr/ ib/2000/ 041200.htm. Accessed on 31 December 2002.

Joes, Anthony James. *America and Guerilla Warfare.* Lexington: University of Kentucky Press, 2000.

_____. *Guerilla Warfare: A Historical, Biographical and Bibliographical Sourcebook.* Westport: Greenwood Press, 1996.

Joint Forces Staff College. *The Joint Staff Officer's Guide 2000.* 2000.

Joint Publication 1-02. *Department of Defense Dictionary of Military and Associated Terms.* 12 April 2001 as amended through 25 September 2002.

Joint Publication 3-0. *Doctrine for Joint Operations.* 10 September 2001.

Joint Publication 3-07. *Joint Doctrine for Military Operations Other than War.* 16 June 1995.

Joint Publication 3-07.1. *Joint Tactics, Techniques, and Procedures (JTTP) for Foreign Internal Defense(FID).* 26 June 1996.

Joint Publication 5-0. *Doctrine for Planning Joint Operations.* 13 April 1995.

Joint Publication 5-00.1. *Joint Doctrine for Campaign Planning.* 25 January 2002.

Kerkvliet, Benedict J. *The Huk Rebellion: A Study of Peasant Revolt in the Philippines.* Berkeley: University of California Press, 1977. Reprint, Lanham: Rowman & Littlefield Publishers, Inc, 2002.

Kipp, Jacob, W. "General-Major A. A. Svechin and Modern Warfare: Military History and Military Theory." In *Strategy,* Aleksandr A. Svechin, ed. Kent D. Lee, 23-56. Minneapolis: East View Publications, 1992.

Kitson, Frank. *Low Intensity Operations: Subversion, Insurgency, Peace-keeping.* Harrisburg: Stackpole Books, 1971.

Lachica, Eduardo. *The Huks: Philippine Agrarian Society in Revolt.* New York: Praeger Publishers, 1971.

Lansdale, Edward G. *In the Midst of Wars: An American's Mission to Southeast Asia.* New York: Harper & Row, Publishers, 1972. Reprint, New York: Fordham University Press, 1991.

Laurie, M.I. "The Operational Level in Low Intensity Conflict," *Low Intensity Conflict and Law Enforcement* 1, no. 3 (Winter 1992): 312-323.

LeoGrande, William M. *Our Own Backyard: The United States in Central America, 1977-1992.* Chapel Hill: The University of North Carolina Press, 1998.

Luvaas, Jay. "Lessons and Lessons Learned: A Historical Perspective." In *The Lessons of Recent Wars in the Third World, Volume I,* ed. Robert E. Harkavy and Stephanie G. Neuman, 51-72. Lexington: Lexington Books, 1985.

Manchester, William. *American Caesar: Douglas MacArthur 1880-1964.* Boston: Little, Brown and Company, 1978.

Mann, Edward C., III, Gary Endersby, and Thomas R. Searle. *Thinking Effects: Effects-Based Methodology for Joint Operations*, CADRE Paper No. 15. Maxwell Air Force Base: Air University Press, 2002.

Manwaring, Max G. and Court Prisk. *El Salvador at War: An Oral History from the 1979 Insurrection to the Present.* Washington, DC: National Defense University Press, 1988.

Manwaring, Max G. *Internal Wars: Rethinking Problem and Response.* Carlisle Barracks: Strategic Studies Institute, U.S. Army War College, September 2001.

_____. "Toward an Understanding of Insurgency Wars: The Paradigm." In *Uncomfortable Wars: Toward a New Paradigm of Low Intensity Conflict,* ed. Max G. Manwaring, 19-28. Westview Studies in Regional Security, ed. Wm. J. Olson. Boulder: Westview Press, 1991.

Marks, Thomas A. "Evaluating Insurgent/Counterinsurgent Performance," *Small Wars and Insurgencies* 11, no. 3 (Winter 2000): 21-46.

Metz, Steven. "A Flame Kept Burning: Counterinsurgency Support After the Cold War," *Parameters* 25, no. 3, (Autumn 1995): 31-41.

_____. *Counterinsurgency: Strategy and the Phoenix of American Capability.* Carlisle Barracks: Strategic Studies Institute, U.S. Army War College, 28 February 1995.

_____. "Counterinsurgent Campaign Planning," *Parameters* 19, no. 3, (September 1989): 60-68.

_____. *The Future of Insurgency.* Carlisle Barracks: Strategic Studies Institute, U.S. Army War College, 10 December 1993.

Mendel, William W. and Floyd T. Banks. "Campaign Planning: Getting it Straight," *Parameters* 18, no. 3, (September 1988): 43-53.

Miller, Thomas E. "The Efficacy of Urban Insurgency in the Modern Era." Masters Thesis, U.S. Army Command and General Staff College, 31 May 2002.

Mintzberg, Henry. *The Rise and Fall of Strategic Planning: Reconceiving Roles for Planning, Plans, Planners.* New York: The Free Press, 1994.

Montgomery, Tommie Sue. *Revolution in El Salvador: From Civil Strife to Civil Peace*, 2d ed. Boulder: Westview Press, 1995.

Morrissey, Michael T. *End State: Relevant in Stability Operations?* Fort Leavenworth, KS: U.S. Army Command and General Staff College, May 2002.

Naveh, Shimon. *In Pursuit of Military Excellence: The Evolution of Operational Theory.* London: Frank Cass, 1997.

Office of the Chief of Army Field Forces, Fort Monroe, Virginia. *Combat Information*, Training Bulletin No.5, 27 September 1951, 1. Quoted in Jay Luvaas, "Lessons and Lessons Learned: A Historical Perspective," in *The Lessons of Recent Wars in the Third World,*

Volume I, ed. Robert E. Harkavy and Stephanie G. Neuman, 51-72. Lexington: Lexington Books, 1985, 66.

O'Neill, Bard E. *Insurgency & Terrorism: Inside Modern Revolutionary Warfare.* Dulles: Brassey's (US), Inc., 1990.

Paget, Julian. *Counter-Insurgency Operations: Techniques of Guerrilla Warfare.* New York: Walker and Company, 1967.

Peterson, A.H., G.C. Reinhard and E.E. Conger, eds. *Symposium on the Role of Airpower in Counterinsurgency and Unconventional Warfare: The Philippine Huk Campaign.* Santa Monica: RAND, RM-3652-PR, July 1963.

Rose, Donald G. "FM 3-0 *Operations*: The Effect of Humanitarian Operations on US Army Doctrine," *Small Wars and Insurgencies* 13, no. 1 (Spring 2002): 57-82.

Romulo, Carlos P. and Marvin D. Gray. *The Magsaysay Story.* New York: The John Day Company, 1956.

Rosello, Victor "Lessons From El Salvador," *Parameters* 23, no. 4 (Winter 1993-94), 100-108.

Sanger, Richard H. *Insurgent Era: New Patterns of Political, Economic, and Social Revolution.* Washington, DC: Potomac Books, Inc., 1967.

Schirmer, Daniel B. and Stephen R. Shalom, eds. *The Philippines Reader: A History of Colonialism, Neocolonialism, Dictatorship and Resistance.* Boston: South End Press, 1987.

Schwarz, Benjamin C. *American Counterinsurgency Doctrine and El Salvador: The Frustrations of Reform and the Illusions of Nation Building.* Santa Monica: RAND, R-4042-USDP, 1991.

Shy, John and Thomas W. Collier. "Revolutionary Warfare." In *Makers of Modern Strategy: From Machiavelli to the Nuclear Age*, ed. Peter Paret, 815-862. Princeton: Princeton University Press, 1986.

Slade, Stuart. "Successful Counter-insurgency: How Thais Burnt the Books and Beat the Guerillas," in *Internal Security & CO-IN,* an editorial supplement to *International Defense Review 22,* (October 1989): 21-25.

Strange, Joe. *Centers of Gravity & Critical Vulnerabilities: Building on the Clausewitizian Foundation So That We Can All Speak the Same Language.* Quantico: Marine Corps University Foundation, 1996.

Summers, Harry G. Jr. "A War Is a War Is a War Is a War." In *Low-Intensity Conflict: The Pattern of Warfare in the Modern World,* ed. Loren B. Thompson, 27-49. Lexington: Lexington Books, 1989.

Svechin, Aleksandr A. *Strategy.* Edited by Kent D. Lee. Minneapolis: East View Publications, 1992.

Taruc, Luis. *He Who Rides the Tiger: The Story of an Asian Guerilla Leader.* New York: Frederick A. Praeger, Publishers, 1967.

Thompson, Leroy. *The Counterinsurgency Manual.* London: Greenhill Books, 2002.

Thompson, Robert. *Defeating Communist Insurgency: Experiences from Malaya and Vietnam.* Studies in International Security: 10. London: MacMillan Press, Ltd., 1966.

Toase, Francis. "The French Experience." In *The Roots of Counter-Insurgency: Armies and Guerilla Warfare, 1900-1945*, ed. Ian F.W. Beckett, 40-59. London: Blanford Press, 1988.

Trinquier, Roger. *Modern Warfare: A French View of Counterinsurgency.* With an introduction by Bernard Fall. Translated by Daniel Lee. New York: Frederick A. Praeger, 1964.

Turabian, Kate L. *A Manual for Writers of Term Papers, Theses, and Dissertations.* 6th ed. Chicago: University of Chicago Press, 1996.

U.S. Census Bureau. "World Population Profile: 1998 – Highlights." Site at http://www.census.gov/ipc/www/wp98001.html. Accessed on 12 December 2002.

U.S. National Security Council Staff. "A Report to the President by the National Security Council with Respect to the Philippines." NSC 84/2. 9 November 1950. In *The Philippines Reader: A History of Colonialism, Neocolonialism, Dictatorship and Resistance*, ed. Daniel B. Schirmer and Stephen R. Shalom, 105-110. Boston: South End Press, 1987.

Waghelstein, John. *El Salvador: Observations and Experiences in Counterinsurgency.* Carlisle Barracks: US Army War College, 1985.

_____, COL (RET), US Army, former CDR, USMILGP, El Salvador from 1982 to 1983. Interview by author, 13 February 2003. Telephonic. Fort Leavenworth, KS.

Winnefeld, James A., Margaret C. Harrell, Robert D. Howe, Arnold Kanter, Brian Nichiporuk, Paul S. Steinberg, Thomas S. Szayna, and Ashley J. Tellis. *Intervention in Intrastate Conflict: Implications for the Army in the Post-Cold War Era.* Santa Monica: RAND, MR-554/1-A, 1995.

Woerner, Frederick F. *Report of the El Salvador Military Strategy Assistance Team (Draft).* Photocopy of a classified report released with excisions under the Freedom of Information Act. San Salvador, 12 September – 8 November 1981. Site at http://www.gwu.edu/~nsarchiv/nsa/DOCUMENT/930325.htm. Accessed on 31 January 2003.

_____, GEN (RET), US Army, former Commander in Chief, US Southern Command. Interview by author, 18 February 2003. Telephonic. Fort Leavenworth, KS.

Valeriano, Napoleon D. and Charles T.R. Bohannan. *Counter-Guerilla Operations: The Philippine Experience.* New York: Frederick A. Praeger, Publisher, 1962.